TURNER **CLASSIC** MOVIES.

CINEMATIC CITIES

New York

TURNER **CLASSIC** MOVIES.

CINEMATIC CITIES

New York

THE BIG APPLE ON THE BIG SCREEN

Christian Blauvelt

Running Press
PHILADELPHIA

Copyright © 2019 by Turner Classic Movies, Inc.
Cover: Getty Image © Silver Screen Collection / Contributor.

Hachette Book Group supports the right to free expression and the value of copyright. The purpose of copyright is to encourage writers and artists to produce the creative works that enrich our culture.

The scanning, uploading, and distribution of this book without permission is a theft of the author's intellectual property. If you would like permission to use material from the book (other than for review purposes), please contact permissions@hbgusa.com. Thank you for your support of the author's rights.

Running Press
Hachette Book Group
1290 Avenue of the Americas, New York, NY 10104
www.runningpress.com
@Running_Press

Printed in China

First Edition: November 2019

Published by Running Press, an imprint of Perseus Books, LLC, a subsidiary of Hachette Book Group, Inc. The Running Press name and logo is a trademark of the Hachette Book Group.

The Hachette Speakers Bureau provides a wide range of authors for speaking events. To find out more, go to www.hachettespeakersbureau.com or call (866) 376-6591.

The publisher is not responsible for websites (or their content) that are not owned by the publisher.

Photo Credits Getty Images/Silver Screen Collection/Contributor.
Maps © Getty Images/Hey Darlin
Print book cover and interior design by Melissa Gerber.

Library of Congress Control Number: 2019943965

ISBNs: 978-0-7624-9543-6 (hardcover), 978-0-7624-9542-9 (ebook)

1010

10 9 8 7 6 5 4 3 2 1

CONTENTS

New York City

INTRODUCTION

NEW YORK CITY IS ONE OF THE GREATEST, most complex characters ever featured in the movies. And it is a character—pulsing with life, changing seemingly from hour to hour, and possessing a personality all its own.

It just so happens that as New York matured into a global capital of culture and commerce, becoming the defining city of the twentieth century and a virtual stand-in for the idea of modernity, the movies came into their own as the century's defining art form as well. The big screen and the Big Apple are indelibly intertwined.

This book attempts a cinematic history of New York City, from the very first movie shot there, by a cameraman for Thomas Edison on May 11, 1896, all the way through the classic Hollywood period and up to *Can You Ever Forgive Me?* and *If Beale Street Could Talk*, two Manhattan-set triumphs from 2018 that seem destined to become classics. But rather than going decade by decade, this book goes neighborhood by neighborhood. If you're a cinephile visiting New York City, this approach will guide your sightseeing, based on your favorite movies. But if you're a New Yorker, this approach enables you to appreciate your surroundings that much more, to truly immerse yourself in the city around you based on the silver screen classics you adore. When you realize that a particular location you visit is actually one from a film you cherish, it's like stepping through the movie screen. And though the city changes so quickly, so much also endures: from the subway vent that caused Marilyn Monroe's white dress to flutter, to the courtyard that inspired Jimmy Stewart's view in *Rear Window* (1954).

This book covers all of Manhattan plus the four outer boroughs. It can't possibly reference every single movie that's been filmed on location here, but if not a completist take, it's an overview to inspire further exploration. Holding this guide in your hands, your personal cinematic journey through New York City begins.

The ON THE TOWN TOUR

Start at the Brooklyn Navy Yard where Gabey, Chip, and Ozzie disembark. It remained an active military shipyard until 1966. It is currently a vibrant industrial park, home to over four hundred businesses. To head for the Brooklyn Bridge from the Navy Yard, walk west on Flushing Avenue and hang a left on Duffield Street. Walk south on Duffield until you reach Tillary Street and keep walking west until you reach the Brooklyn Bridge pedestrian entrance.

On the Town is one of the most beloved movies set in New York City, maybe because it seems like it's so in love with the city itself: shot partly on location in the Big Apple, something extremely rare for any musical in 1949, it tells the story of three sailors, Gabey (Gene Kelly), Chip (Frank Sinatra), and Ozzie (Jules Munshin). They're on leave for just one glorious day—but do they ever see and do a lot! *On the Town* presents New York as a place of discovery, opportunity, and romance—and that transformation, of both the city and of the visitor, is inevitable. The film opens with an energetic montage set to Leonard Bernstein's "New York, New York." (This is the one that goes "New York, New York, it's a wonderful town / The Bronx is up and the Battery's down.") In an opening sequence of just three minutes, Gabey, Chip, and Ozzie sightsee and sing their way through a whirlwind tour of some of the city's most treasured—and tourist-friendly—landmarks. The montage shows their itinerary so clearly, you can replicate it yourself! Here's the route to follow to take in everything the sailors visited during "New York, New York."

Cross the Brooklyn Bridge by foot. The bridge's pedestrian walkway begins at the intersection of Tillary Street and Boerum Place and ends at the northeast edge of City Hall Park on Centre Street. It takes about thirty minutes to walk from Brooklyn to Manhattan.

Head south along Centre Street until it becomes Park Row and merges with Broadway. Keep heading south on Broadway until you hit Trinity Church, which opened in 1846 and was the tallest structure in the city until the Brooklyn Bridge opened in 1883.

Backtrack along the route you took from City Hall, then cross to the east side of Columbus Park. Walk down Bayard Street, Elizabeth Street, Mott Street, and Mulberry Street to sample gastronomic delights in Chinatown— then keep walking north on Mulberry past Canal Street and you'll enter Little Italy.

Take the number 4 or 5 subway trains to Bowling Green and
get the ferry to the Statue of Liberty from Battery Park.

Since the Third Avenue El tracks that the sailors visit no longer exist, do the next best thing by taking a cab to Chelsea's High Line. Then climb up and walk this elevated railroad track that was converted into a beautiful park in 2009.

From the southernmost terminus of the High Line at Gansevoort Street, walk to Washington Square Park and run through the Arch, then drive past the historic Helmsley Building at Grand Central Station, and head all the way up to Riverside Park to visit Grant's Tomb and Riverside Church, the tallest church in the United States.

Hire a horse-drawn carriage on Central Park South and have your driver take you as close as you can to Cleopatra's Needle past Seventy-Ninth Street, followed by a spin on a bicycle and a run across the Sheep Meadow.

Take a cab down Fifth Avenue and get out just past Fifty-First Street. Gaze at Lee Lawrie's *Atlas* statue at Rockefeller Center, then ride an elevator all the way to the Top of the Rock for one of the best views of the city.

Check out Paul Manship's statue *Prometheus*, depicting the Greek Titan who first gave fire to man, over which the Rockefeller Center Christmas Tree is placed each year, and you'll have visited everything Gabey, Chip, and Ozzie see during the opening of *On the Town*.

The On the Town Tour | 7

The *STATUE of* LIBERTY

The Statue of Liberty has become cinematic shorthand for the immigrant experience—even for immigrants from another world.

"You sail into the harbor, and Staten Island is on your left, and then you see the Statue of Liberty. This is what everyone in the world dreams of when they think about New York. And I thought, 'My God, I'm in Heaven. I'll be dancing down Fifth Avenue like Fred Astaire with Ginger Rogers.'"

—Frank McCourt

APOLOGIES TO THE *MALTESE FALCON*, but it's Lady Liberty who's truly "the stuff dreams are made of." For countless immigrants dreaming of a better life in America, this beacon of freedom towering over New York Harbor was the first thing they saw when they arrived.

Standing 151 feet and 1 inch, or 305 feet and 1 inch if you include the pedestal, this copper statue was a gift from France to the United States in celebration of the one hundredth anniversary of American independence—though it was only dedicated ten years later, in 1886. The funny thing is that, nine years after that, cinema itself would also be France's gift: in 1895, the Lumière brothers created the motion picture–filming and projection techniques that most agree was the official beginning of the movies. And if the movies teach us "how to desire," as philosopher Slavoj Žižek has said, the Statue of Liberty teaches us *what* to desire: the dual freedom to be who you are . . . and to attempt to become whatever you wish to be. It's the American Dream itself, a symbol of hope whether you're an immigrant from Königsberg or Krypton.

ELLIS ISLAND

For tourists from Manhattan, the Statue of Liberty, nestled on top of Bedloe's Island (renamed Liberty Island in 1956), is a short ferry ride away. For the twelve million immigrants who would pass through nearby Ellis Island, the checkpoint from 1892 to 1954 for all foreigners seeking asylum in America via New York, the Statue of Liberty marked the beginning of their life as new Americans—much as it did for young Vito Andolini (Oreste Baldini) in *The Godfather Part II* (1974). The words by poet Emma Lazarus inscribed on Lady Liberty's pedestal—"Give me your tired, your poor, your huddled masses yearning to breathe free"—could serve as a mission statement for America itself.

Vito Andolini, soon to be renamed Vito Corleone, gazes at the Statue of Liberty from his quarantine room at Ellis Island in *The Godfather Part II*.

Fanny Brice, though not an immigrant, was certainly an embodiment of the American Dream. In *Funny Girl* (1968), Barbra Streisand plays Brice and ends her song "Don't Rain on My Parade" with a note of ecstatic hope and yearning aboard a tugboat passing in front of the statue. On a more somber note, it looms over Rose (Kate Winslet) in *Titanic* (1997) when she returns to New York aboard the RMS *Carpathia* following the sinking of the doomed liner. The Statue of Liberty marked the end of her harrowing journey and the beginning of a new one, too.

Barbra Streisand sings a showstopper in front of the Statue of Liberty in *Funny Girl*—it represents her hopes and dreams.

LAND OF UNCERTAINTIES

Charlie Chaplin directed and starred in 1917's *The Immigrant*, in which his Little Tramp character passes through Ellis Island on his journey to a better life. And on their way, they pass by the Statue of Liberty. Though his clothes are ratty, the fact he wears a suit, with a waistcoat, tie, cane, and hat, builds an element of the aspirational into the very idea of the Little Tramp. And through his good manners and concern for his fellow man, the Little Tramp also embodies something countless immigrants have also: dreams of a better future, yes, but dignity in the present, too.

Charlie Chaplin was an immigrant to America himself, having grown up on London's South Bank. He'd stay in the United States for many years after he made his first short for Keystone Studios in 1914.

GATEWAY TO A NEW LIFE

Ellis Island was a scary place for many immigrants, though. They could be quarantined for weeks or longer while they were screened for diseases. Young Vito Andolini in *The Godfather Part II* is accidentally renamed Vito Corleone by an immigration officer simply because his hometown was Corleone, Sicily. In the 2013 film *The Immigrant*, director James Gray showed that sometimes accommodations could be made for the health and well-being of immigrants; however, in one moving scene, Enrico Caruso visits Ellis Island to sing for all those hoping to be let into America.

Young Vito had to leave Sicily to save his life after a Mafia boss killed his parents—but America would present its own hardships, such as Ellis Island's rigorous quarantines.

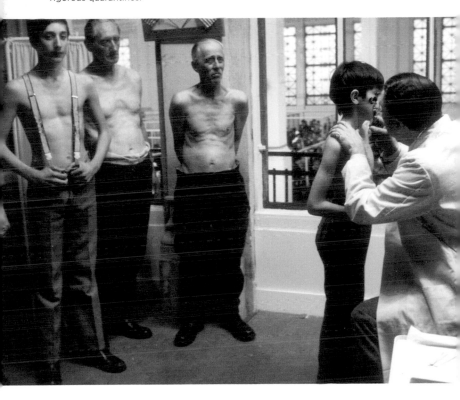

Spotlight on Saboteur (1942)

Alfred Hitchcock applied his "wrong-man-on-the-run" formula to this 1942 thriller about Nazi spies in America wanting to foment dissent and cripple the US war effort. It ends with a dramatic showdown on the Statue of Liberty as the villain (Norman Lloyd, who turned 104 in 2018) stumbles off the balcony surrounding Lady Liberty's torch, with only the hero (Bob Cummings) holding on to him by a thread. Literally.

Norman Lloyd's villain, a Nazi saboteur named Fry, escapes Manhattan after a shootout at Radio City Music Hall by taking the ferry to the statue.

Fry knows Kane (Bob Cummings) is on his tail. Some shots were filmed at the statue, but most were accomplished via matte paintings and forced-perspective composites.

Fry confronts the hero's ally, Pat (Priscilla Lane), in the observation deck of Lady Liberty's crown. The chase then moves to the torch itself.

The final showdown on the Statue's torch may seem far-fetched, but in fact the torch had been damaged in real life from an act of terrorism conducted by German saboteurs in 1916 during World War I. The torch has been closed to the public ever since.

WHEN THE AMERICAN DREAM
BECOMES A NIGHTMARE

Because the Statue of Liberty is not just a symbol of America but of freedom itself, filmmakers sometimes like to show that something horrible has happened to it as an indication that the world has fallen into darkness and despair. Lady Liberty is toppled off her pedestal after the aliens destroy New York City in the disaster epic *Independence Day* (1996). Only her torch remains above the water after catastrophic climate change has caused seawater to rise dramatically in *A.I.: Artificial Intelligence* (2001)—a visual virtually repeated just three years later on the poster for *The Day After Tomorrow* (2004), with the risen sea frozen over. (The image of just Liberty's torch is actually what New Yorkers first saw of the statue—before the rest was assembled, just the torch was on display in Madison Square Park from 1876 to 1882.) And yet she somehow endures intact, though covered by a strange postapocalyptic beach, long after New York vanished and human civilization itself disappeared in *Planet of the Apes* (1968).

Charlton Heston discovers a shocking truth about the strange world on which he's crash-landed in *Planet of the Apes*.

The Twilight Zone creator and master of the jaw-dropping twist, Rod Serling, co-wrote the unforgettable ending of *Planet of the Apes.*

Planet of the Apes made the destruction of the Statue of Liberty a cinematic shorthand for end-times hellishness—including for director Drew Goddard, whose poster for his monster movie *Cloverfield* (2008) showed Liberty's head chomped off.

Lady Liberty ran afoul of a monster in *Cloverfield.*

LOWER MANHATTAN

Jane Fonda's Corie searches for her husband, Paul (Robert Redford), at Washington Square Park in *Barefoot in the Park* (1967).

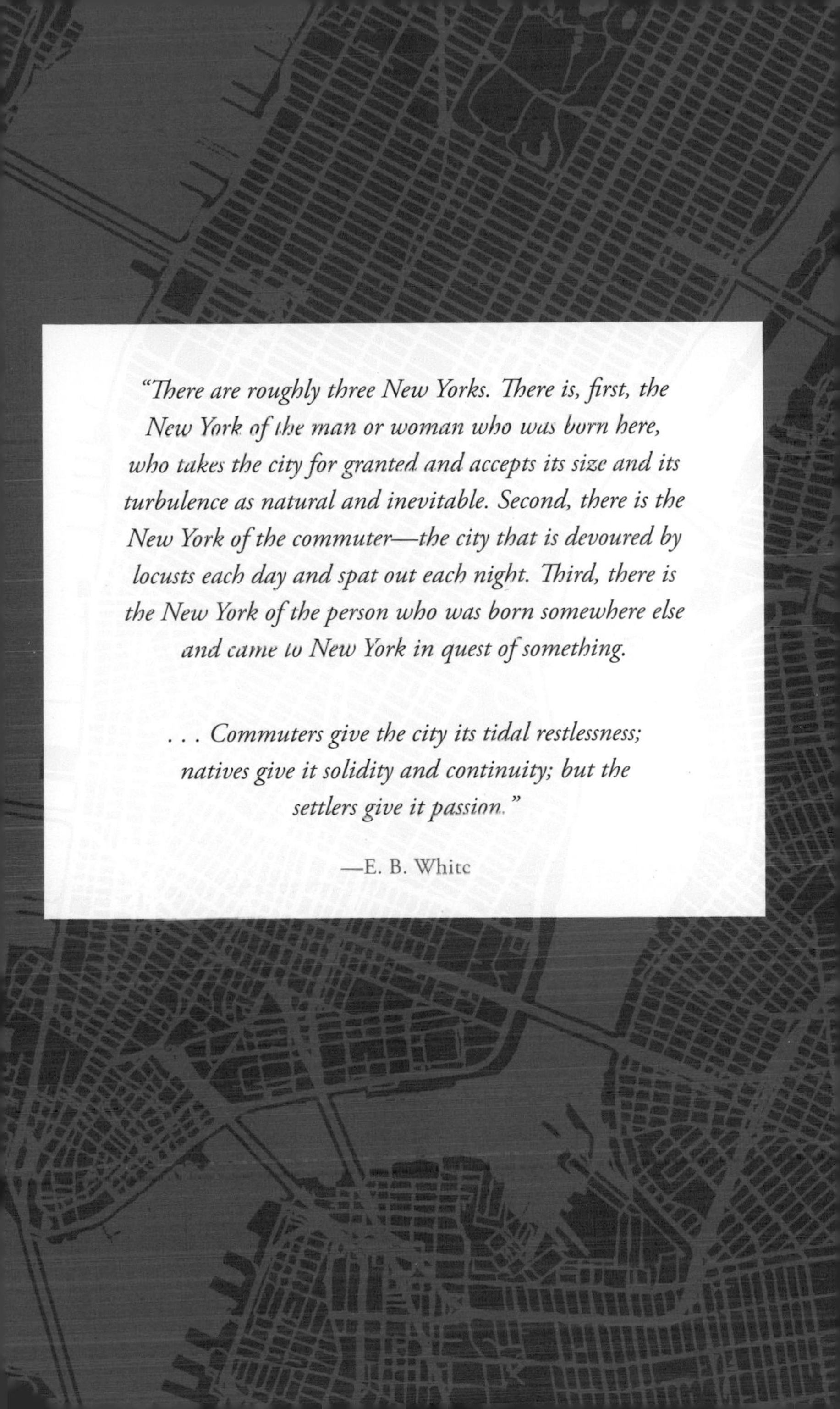

"There are roughly three New Yorks. There is, first, the New York of the man or woman who was born here, who takes the city for granted and accepts its size and its turbulence as natural and inevitable. Second, there is the New York of the commuter—the city that is devoured by locusts each day and spat out each night. Third, there is the New York of the person who was born somewhere else and came to New York in quest of something.

. . . Commuters give the city its tidal restlessness; natives give it solidity and continuity; but the settlers give it passion."

—E. B. White

MORE OFTEN THAN NOT, WHEN DREAMERS
come to New York on a quest, as White, the longtime editor of the *New Yorker* and author of *Charlotte's Web* and *Stuart Little*, put it, they settle in Lower Manhattan. Or at least until the last decade or two they did. Anyone hoping to "make it" in New York (because if you can make it here you'll make it anywhere, to paraphrase Fred Ebb's lyrics to the iconic "Theme from *New York, New York*") might find Lower Manhattan's ever-skyrocketing rents a little too steep for a first apartment in New York these days. But until the early 2000s, before they had completely become millionaire playgrounds, the neighborhoods of Greenwich Village, the Lower East Side, and Chelsea were magnets for anyone low on cash but high on dreams.

GREENWICH VILLAGE

We're on a journey with a dreamer first arriving in New York in the final moments of Greta Gerwig's *Lady Bird* (2017), set in 2003, when, suitcase in hand, eighteen-year-old Lady Bird McPherson (Saoirse Ronan) emerges from the West Fourth Street subway station on Sixth Avenue—she must have taken the A train directly from JFK airport—to start college life in Manhattan, maybe at nearby New York University. We see her, eyes raised and mouth open, taking in all of New York with wonder. Like so many students in Lower Manhattan, she'll likely become a regular at the Strand Book Store at 12th and Broadway, which can be glimpsed from the window of the apartment where Monty Woolley's Professor Wutheridge lives in *The Bishop's Wife* (1947). It was Lady Bird's dream to go to school here and be around like-minded artistic souls, though really that dream is a stepping stone to other dreams: success as a writer, validation of her voice and point of view, maybe even fame.

That's the thing about New York. Dreams bring you here, but then those dreams lead to other dreams—and those are the ones that keep you here. For those just starting out, Greenwich Village is a particularly fertile place for ambitions to take root. Lady Bird came there for school; Corie and Paul Bratter, newlyweds played by Jane Fonda and Robert Redford in *Barefoot in the Park*, came there for the cheap rent. They start their conjugal life in a top-floor apartment in a creaky brownstone. No elevator, of course. This walk-up doesn't even have heat to get them through the winter. It's a level of "roughing it" that's almost like camping, but it's what they, and so many other recent graduates, endure before their careers can take off.

Lower Manhattan has historically been the very definition of the "melting pot," the uniquely American notion of people from all different backgrounds, ethnicities, religions, and political persuasions coming together in an exchange that ends up blending identities and shifting boundaries. That diversity is part of why Lady Bird wanted to come to New York—but it was also part of what motivated Louise Bryant, played by Diane Keaton, in *Reds* (1981), to arrive in Greenwich Village from her home in Oregon, to share in the trade of ideas with other writers and reporters as World War I raged across Europe. She eventually married journalist and communist organizer John Reed, played by Warren Beatty, and followed him to Russia to report on the Bolshevik Revolution and its aftermath. This factual historical drama keeps expanding and expanding until it's incredibly epic in scope. But it's initially an intimate character study about two people falling in love and their interactions with socialist dissidents, such as Emma Goldman, and socially conscious artists like the playwright Eugene O'Neill (Jack Nicholson) in the bohemian garrets of Greenwich Village.

Where to Eat:
Katz's Delicatessen

Immigrants settling in Lower Manhattan found solace in their compatriots from the Old Country. Restaurants, delis, butcher shops—any place at all that sold food—could be a meeting place for these new Americans who shared a common ancestry.

One focal point for Jewish American life on the Lower East Side, was (and is) Katz's Delicatessen, first founded by the Iceland brothers in 1888. This Houston Street staple remains as bustling as ever today—expect a twenty-minute wait even for a late lunch around 3:00 p.m. and up to an hour before you're seated around noon or dinnertime—because it boasts the best pastrami in the city. Meg Ryan's Sally Albright in *When Harry Met Sally . . .* (1989) sure thought so. Or at least the diners at nearby tables must have assumed she did, in what is one of the most iconic moments from a romantic comedy ever.

A sign hangs over the table where Harry and Sally were sitting at Katz's Delicatessen, so you can re-create her ecstatic moment for yourself, if you're so inclined.

LITTLE ITALY

Food brought people together in other ways for Vito Corleone. On Mott Street in Little Italy, Vito (Robert De Niro) opened his olive-oil shop in *The Godfather Part II*. It was merely a front for him to develop the network of favors and debts that would form the basis of his Mafia empire. Mott Street and nearby Mulberry Street are the heart of this community south of Houston, where so many immigrants from Italy settled. Much of the character of Little Italy has been absorbed into the ultraexpensive neighborhood of SoHo (for "South of Houston"), meaning that it's full of boutique shops for designer labels and not as many signs of the countless dreamers who once settled here hoping for a better life. But there are still some locations you can see that were featured in *The Godfather* (1972). St. Patrick's Old Cathedral on Mulberry Street is where the baptism occurs at the end of the first movie, when director Francis Ford Coppola cuts between the holy ritual and gory images of the many enemies Michael Corleone (Al Pacino) has ordered to be gunned down while he's in church with his newborn son.

A year later, Martin Scorsese would film a scene in *Mean Streets* (1973) at Old St. Patrick's Cathedral in which Harvey Keitel and Robert De Niro's characters have a conversation. Then Coppola and Pacino returned to film at St. Patrick's Old Cathedral for *The Godfather Part III* (1990) for a scene in which Michael is inducted

From a simple olive-oil shop on Mott Street, Vito Corleone (Robert De Niro) would go on to build a crime empire in *The Godfather Part II*.

into a papal order. And it's nearby outside on Mulberry Street where, after a stunning shootout, Andy Garcia's Vincent Mancini kills Joe Mantegna's Joey Zasa. Head farther downtown still, all the way to 33 Liberty Street, to see the Federal Reserve Bank, the exterior of which is used as the building where the meeting of the Five Families occurs to prevent a "war" in the first film. It's also where the ransom money that's to be paid to subway hijacker Robert Shaw is counted and collected in *The Taking of Pelham One Two Three* (1974).

THE WORLD TRADE CENTER

You can't embark on a cinematic tour of New York City without taking a moment to acknowledge the Twin Towers. From when they opened on April 4, 1973, to when they fell in the horrific violence of September 11, 2001, they were a dramatic punctuation mark to the New York City skyline that conveyed power and wealth—and a sense that we really could touch the sky. It'll take years, if not decades, for the new skyscraper that sits nearby, One World Trade Center, to be featured in as many films as its two predecessors.

Before the Twin Towers had even opened they were the site of the finale of the song "All for the Best" in the movie version of the hit Broadway musical *Godspell* (1973). They had previously been featured, unfinished and still under construction, in *Klute* and *The French Connection*, both released in 1971. They were then scaled by the giant ape in John Guillermin's 1976 remake of *King Kong*, Jessica Lange clutched in his grip. In *Trading Places* (1983), the World Trade Center is where Dan Aykroyd's Louis Winthorpe III and street hustler Billy Ray Valentine (Eddie Murphy) launch their scheme to impoverish the Duke brothers (Ralph Bellamy and Don Ameche) who've been meddling in their lives. Kevin McCallister ascends to the 107th floor and then to the rooftop observation deck of the South Tower in *Home Alone 2: Lost in New York* (1992).

After 9/11, many appearances of the Twin Towers were edited out of movies and TV shows currently in production, such as *Friends* (the World Trade Center appeared in the original opening credits of the sitcom) and *Sex and the City*. Most famously, a 2001 teaser for Sam

Raimi's first *Spider-Man* film (2002) featured the superhero trapping bank robbers who flew away from their crime in a helicopter in a giant web he'd spun between the Twin Towers. Sony, the studio behind the film, fearing the trailer was now in poor taste, immediately pulled it. Some World Trade Center–adjacent sites still exist, however, such as the World Financial Center at 225 Liberty Street and its famous Winter Garden featured in Brian De Palma's *The Bonfire of the Vanities* (1990). It was heavily damaged during 9/11 but reopened less than a year afterward.

CLUBS AND COVENS

Lower Manhattan is a place for beginnings, for "starting out." Certainly that's been the case for the many musicians who settled here and first honed their tuneful chops in the nightclubs of Greenwich Village and the Lower East Side. CBGB, located until its closing in 2006 at the intersection of Broadway and the Bowery, was the heart of the punk explosion in the late 1970s and '80s, featuring performances by Patti Smith, the Ramones, Talking Heads, Television, Suicide, and Blondie. Ivan Král and Amos Poe's documentary *The Blank Generation* (1976) reveals footage of these artists before they hit stardom and gives you a sense of what CBGB would have been like. It's where Dianne Wiest takes Woody Allen to hear rockers the 39 Steps (yep, named after the Hitchcock film) in *Hannah and Her Sisters* (1986) and gushes her love for songs about extraterrestrial life.

Oscar Isaac's struggling folk musician Llewyn Davis performs at the Gaslight Café, which was only open from 1958 to 1971, but shaped American culture like few other clubs in history: it was the petri dish for the folk music explosion of the early 1960s, including for Dave Van Ronk, the real-life inspiration for Isaac's character in *Inside Llewyn Davis* (2013). It also hosted young Bruce Springsteen, Jimi Hendrix, Eric Clapton, Bonnie Raitt, and Charles Mingus—plus, Bob Dylan, who only shows up at the very end of *Inside Llewyn Davis*, and would spring to fame from the Gaslight Café in a meteoric way that would elude Davis (and Van Ronk). Today, a craft cocktail bar called the Up & Up occupies its site at 116 MacDougal Street. You can imagine when you visit the Up & Up, though, that the Gaslight Café would also have been the type of cool-cat joint where Jack Lemmon's warlock plays the bongos in *Bell, Book and Candle* (1958), a film that reflects another movement to which the Village gave birth: the Beats. These countercultural precursors to the hippies, beatniks included poet Allen Ginsberg (a regular at the Gaslight Café), and authors William S. Burroughs and Jack Kerouac. Two landmark films about the Beats were set in their Village milieu, Shirley Clarke's *The Connection* (1961), and Robert Frank and Albert Leslie's *Pull My Daisy* (1959), filmed at a loft on Fourth Avenue and Twelfth Street. The fact that Lemmon's bongo-playing Beat in *Bell, Book and Candle* is a warlock should give a sense of how much Beats were regarded as "the other" by mainstream American society—the suspicion was that they could be capable of literally anything. Of course it's an extremely charming portrayal in *Bell, Book and Candle*—an

The live music hot spot where Jack Lemmon plays the bongos is called the Zodiac Club in *Bell, Book and Candle*. It's similar to what the Gaslight Café would have been like when it opened in 1958, also the year the film was released.

Mary (Kim Hunter), haunted by the murder she's just witnessed, rides the subway in a daze, making a complete circuit, in *The Seventh Victim*. When she returns to the stop where she got on, the murdered man "boards" the train, assisted by his murderers.

extremely charming film, overall—but that association of the counterculture with the occult was not accidental, nor was it the first time it had been expressed onscreen. In Mark Robson's horror film *The Seventh Victim* (1943), a girl named Mary (Kim Hunter) looks for her sister, who has vanished from her apartment in Greenwich Village, and it seems has been spirited away by a group of Village sophisticates who are also devil worshippers. Mary befriends a failed poet who helps in her quest to find her sister. He's a regular patron of the Caffe Dante at 79–81 MacDougal Street, which was founded in 1915 and still remains open for business today. It's definitely the kind of place where you might imagine meeting a poet who knows a thing or two about the occult. As another option, consider getting some refreshment just a few doors down at Caffe Reggio at 119 MacDougal Street, where Llewyn Davis meets Carey Mulligan's fellow folk singer, Jean, for coffee.

The strivers who live in Greenwich Village are not the types to

Jimmy Stewart plays a guy who falls under the literal
spell of Kim Novak's witch in *Bell, Book and Candle*, set in
Greenwich Village at the height of the Beat movement.

own cars or even have a lot of loose cash for taxis—this is a place where everyone rides the subway. Today, though the subway system is among the safest in the world, there can still be something a little eerie about standing in such close proximity to total strangers. Everyone's tightly packed yet you get the sense that no one is really noticing each other. It's that feeling that Kim Hunter's Mary experiences, along with a shiver of terror, when she rides the subway out of Greenwich Village just after she's witnessed a private detective she's hired get murdered. She's sitting in a relatively empty car, when three men get on at a station. Two of them are very carefully attending to the third. No wonder, the third man is the private detective Mary saw murdered—these are his killers and they're propping him up like he's still alive, knowing full well that, this being New York, no one on the subway will notice.

Spotlight on Rear Window (1954)

In New York City, murder is best carried out in the open. That's certainly what Lars Thorwald (Raymond Burr), traveling salesman, thought in Alfred Hitchcock's 1954 masterpiece about a man who kills his wife in their Greenwich Village apartment late one night, then, curtains left undrawn, begins disposing of her effects. Of course Jimmy Stewart's photographer L. B. Jefferies, laid up with a broken leg and bored with nothing else to do, is watching. The movie has an extraordinary sense of atmosphere, with a layered soundtrack meant to give the impression of all the ambient noise you'd really hear living in a Village apartment that overlooks a picturesque multilevel courtyard. You hear the music a dancer across the way plays for her calisthenics, radio ads, the tinkling of a musician's piano, the honking of cars from the street across the courtyard, across which you can see just the corner table of a little café. This aural collage makes the set feel much bigger. And yes, this is a set—the largest in Paramount's history—built entirely on a soundstage with Jefferies's apartment overlooking the courtyard and apartment building across the way, all meticulously crafted to look like it's really been filmed at 125 West Ninth Street, the location mentioned in the film. That address is fictional; go there and you will not see anything that looks like what you see in the film. But, just a few blocks away is 125 Christopher Street, which, though not the address listed in the film, was indeed, according to *New York Post* film critic Lou Lumenick and film historian Donald Spoto, the visual inspiration for the courtyard.

Hitchcock wanted maximum authenticity in the construction of the apartment buildings Jefferies gazes upon across his courtyard: he insisted that each apartment—twelve in total—have running water and electricity, which he proudly showed off to journalists visiting the set.

A magazine photographer who broke his leg while shooting a wreck on a racetrack, Jefferies lives in the Village because he sees himself as a no-frills artist, while his girlfriend, Lisa (Grace Kelly), is part of the posh society set of Midtown.

In his legendary book-length interview with François Truffaut, Hitchcock said he based *Rear Window* on a real-life crime in which a woman was attacked in a courtyard, in full view of her neighbors, and no one reported the crime.

THE HOTEL CHELSEA
222 West Twenty-Third Street

Go fourteen blocks north of where *Rear Window* is supposed to take place and you'll enter the neighborhood of Chelsea, long the heart of the gay community of New York City. During the '60s much of the artistic life of Lower Manhattan moved from the Village to up here. A particular hot spot was the Hotel Chelsea. This unassuming Victorian residence opened in 1884 as one of New York City's first coop apartment buildings, but after some years of financial distress, it began to allow shorter stays as well and become known as a hotel. In the days after the RMS *Titanic* sank in the early hours of April 15, 1912, several survivors who were picked up by the RMS *Carpathia* stayed at the Hotel Chelsea, at the expense of the White Star Line, while officials dealt with the aftermath of the disaster—others were taken straight to nearby St. Vincent's Hospital, which closed in 2010. One of those survivors, Dorothy Gibson, starred in a short film about the sinking, made just weeks after it occurred. She reenacted her experience of the tragedy via the melodramatic silent-film poses of *Saved from the Titanic* (1912), the ten-minute film she wrote herself and filmed across the Hudson at Éclair Film Company's studio in Fort Lee, New Jersey, and aboard a ship set for scrap in New York Harbor. The twenty-two-year-old Gibson had been returning from a vacation with her mother in Italy. Passage aboard the *Titanic* was the fastest way back to New York to start work on a six-picture deal she had for Éclair. For the film she wore a white evening dress covered with a white cardigan polo coat—the same outfit she was wearing when she got into Lifeboat No. 7, the first launched, following the ship striking an iceberg while she was playing bridge in the first-class lounge. Alas, the film, which was first shown on May 14, 1912, and condemned by the *New York Dramatic Mirror* as "revolting" in the way Gibson had "commercialized her good fortune," was lost two years later, when the only prints were destroyed in a fire at Éclair Studios.

The Hotel Chelsea's role as a refuge for *Titanic* survivors isn't talked about as much as one might think, but perhaps that's simply because so very much else happened there in the following decades.

Andy Warhol and Paul Morrissey shot their film *Chelsea Girls* (1966) there. Around three-and-a-half hours, the film depicts, via split screen, the comings and goings at the hotel of various Warhol superstars, including Nico. Keep an eye out for Marie Menken, an accomplished experimental filmmaker in her own right, as Mother. Kenneth Anger once suggested that Edward Albee based the character ultimately played by Elizabeth Taylor in *Who's Afraid of Virginia Woolf?* (1966) on Menken. Following *Chelsea Girls*, Leonard Cohen had an affair with Janis Joplin at the Hotel Chelsea in 1968. During their stay they may have crossed paths with fellow resident Arthur C. Clarke, who wrote *2001: A Space Odyssey* (1968) there. Clarke developed his novel in conjunction with Stanley Kubrick, and it was only released after the film came out.

The Hotel Chelsea is most notorious for a tragedy that took place there that was immortalized in Alex Cox's *Sid & Nancy* (1986). On October 12, 1978, Nancy Spungen, the twenty-year-old girl-friend of former Sex Pistols bassist Sid Vicious, was found dead of a single stab wound underneath the sink in the room they shared to-gether. Vicious was immediately arrested for her murder; after being let out on bail he died of a heroin overdose four months later, at age twenty-one. No one knows for certain what happened. Some think it's possible their drug dealer may have been the one to kill Spungen. Cox cast Gary Oldman as Vicious and Chloe Webb as Spungen in his film, which does indeed, conspiracy theories aside, depict Vicious stabbing Spungen to death. The Hotel Chelsea reopened in 2019 after an eight-year restoration.

Travel south to Union Square and near its southwest corner is where Biograph Studios once stood at 11 East Fourteenth Street. It's a modern office and residential building today, but Biograph was housed in a converted brownstone on this site from 1906 to 1913. It was where D. W. Griffith first cut his teeth as a filmmaker after being turned down for work by Edison Studios, which had a glass-enclosed rooftop studio at 41 East Twenty-First Street. (At that Edison Studios location, some of the interior scenes of Edwin S. Porter's *The Great Train Robbery* were filmed in 1903, with the exteriors filmed in New

Jersey.) In 1908, his first year as a director, Griffith directed forty-nine short subjects. He'd make hundreds more before leaving Biograph in 1913 to found his own production company and eventually make *The Birth of a Nation* (1915).

WASHINGTON SQUARE PARK

If just one place had to stand in for all of Lower Manhattan, it would have to be Washington Square Park. This 9.75-acre rectangle, built around a circular fountain and punctuated on its north side by the iconic Washington Square Arch—built in 1892 in the style of the Arc de Triomphe to celebrate the centennial of George Washington's presidency—was an urban oasis well before Central Park was ever conceived. It's a place where you can sit on a bench to take in the air and find yourself in a heated political debate with a total stranger before long, where all manner of live music acts can be found playing, and where, as depicted in the child prodigy movie *Searching for Bobby Fischer* (1993), people congregate at wooden tables at the park's southwest corner to have spirited chess matches.

Washington Square has a fascinating history. What constitutes the park today was once the site of the first African American settlement in what would become the United States: the Dutch colonial leaders of New Amsterdam gave parcels of land here to freed and partially freed slaves in 1643, in part, hoping that these black settlers would be a buffer between them and the Lenape Native Americans. It continued to be a black community even after the English ousted the Dutch in 1664 and changed the name of the city from New Amsterdam to New York—but after a suppressed slave rebellion in 1712 this early black community was dissolved, its residents scattered. From then on, the area remained undeveloped. Newgate Prison was built on the Hudson on what would later be Tenth Street, perhaps dissuading people from building nearby—Greenwich Village, still very separate from the city of New York, which was mostly a small area around Wall Street, continued to live up to its original Dutch name *Groenwijck*, or "Green District." People convicted of crimes in New York City would be shipped up the Hudson to Newgate Prison, which is the origin of the penal slang "sent up the river." After it closed in 1829, Greenwich Village experienced rapid growth. The wealthy wanted some distance from the hustle and bustle of the city below, so they began their ever-increasing exodus uptown. In 1826, city officials had laid out the rectangular plot that would become Washington Square Park as a militia parade ground, for irregular troops to drill for the common defense. On its northern edge, wealthy new residents built a row of Greek revival houses; it's in one of these houses, and around the 1830s or '40s, that William Wyler's *The Heiress* (1949) takes place. The film is based on Henry James's early novel *Washington Square*, from 1880, and is about a young woman (Olivia de Havilland) who faces heart-

Robert Redford's Paul stumbles by Washington Square Park's statue of Alexander Holley, the man responsible for kicking off much of American steel production, in *Barefoot in the Park*.

breaking rejection at the hands of a suitor and then opts for revenge when he reenters her life. "Yes, I can be cruel," she says near the end of the film. "I've been taught by masters."

On a more lighthearted note, Washington Square Park is the one of the title in *Barefoot in the Park*. Jane Fonda's Corie wants her new husband, Paul (Robert Redford), to lighten up, to be more spontaneous, more of a free spirit. Why wouldn't he ever do something wild and crazy like go walking barefoot in Washington Square Park? At the end of the film, after Paul has walked out on Corie in a huff, she finds him, shirt untucked, stumbling through the park barefoot in a drunken stupor. She finally got what she wanted. Or did she?

The story of a spinster, Olivia de Havilland, who pins her romantic hopes on a man who turns out to be a cad, Montgomery Clift, *The Heiress* won de Havilland her second Academy Award.

While in Lower Manhattan, Keep an Eye Out for . . .

The Broad Street subway station

Patrick Swayze's and Tony Goldwyn's characters climb its stairs out and onto Wall Street in *Ghost* (1990). Standing at the intersection of Broad and Wall Streets, like they did, and looking west, you'll see the historic Trinity Church, where Alexander Hamilton is buried. Remarkably, this shot is a mirror of one nearly identical in *Force of Evil* (1948), which has the same setup and view of Trinity Church. New York City is constantly changing, but this is an example of a view that has pretty much remained unaltered even through today.

Nearby you'll find the once-violent Five Points neighborhood, the place where many Irish immigrants settled in the mid-1800s and memorably depicted in Martin Scorsese's *Gangs of New York* (2002). Little from that time remains, but if you want to visit the Five Points, know that the neighborhood is bounded by Canal Street to the north, the Bowery to the east, Park Row to the south, and Centre Street to the west. Bordering the Five Points on the west is the New York City Hall and Tweed Courthouse, so named after corrupt nineteenth century political boss William M. Tweed, played in *Gangs of New York* by Jim Broadbent.

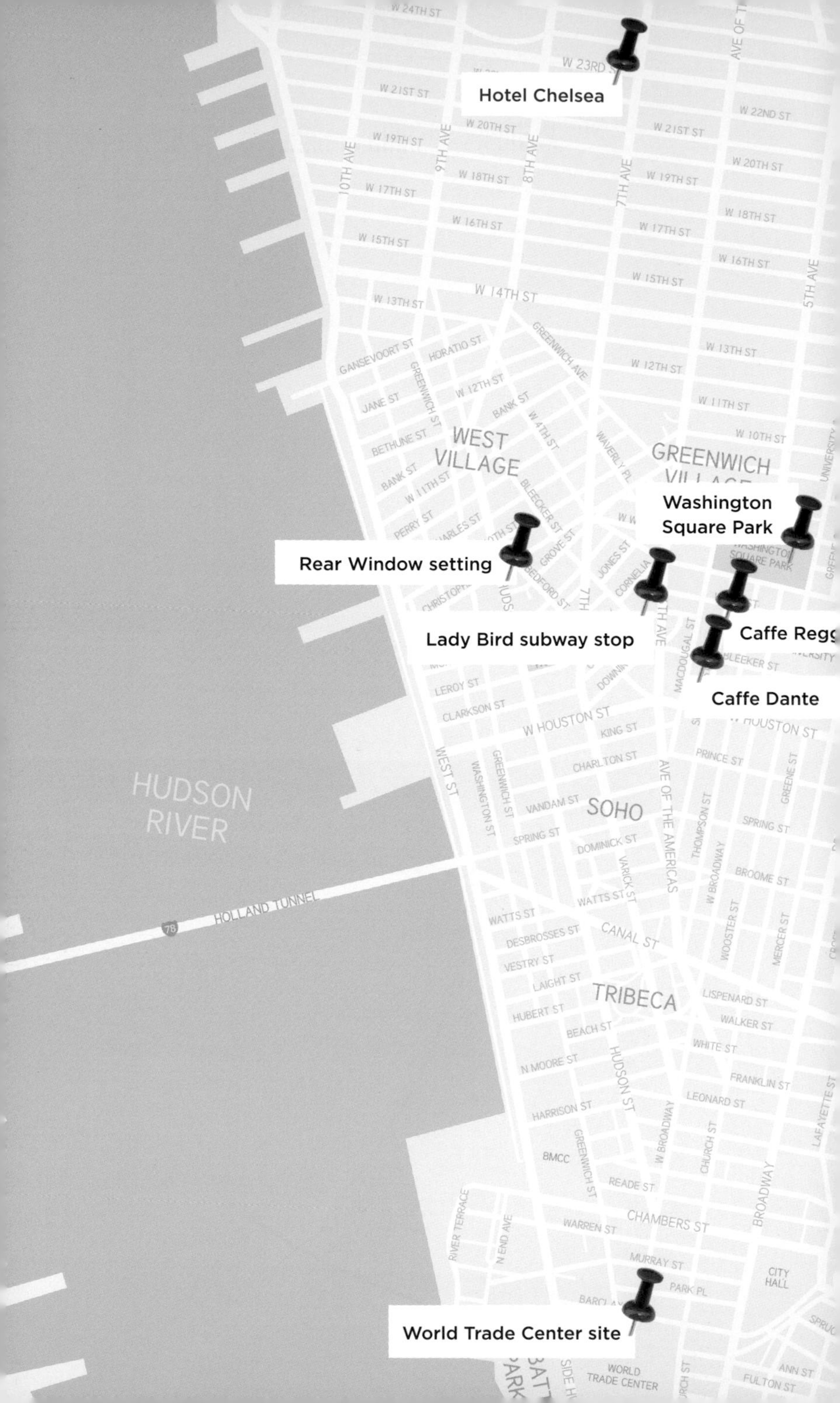

Hotel Chelsea

Washington
Square Park

Rear Window setting

Lady Bird subway stop

Caffe Regg[io]

Caffe Dante

World Trade Center site

WEST
VILLAGE

GREENWICH
VILLAGE

HUDSON
RIVER

HOLLAND TUNNEL

SOHO

TRIBECA

BMCC

CITY
HALL

MIDTOWN MANHATTAN

TOW AWAY ZONE

City

The Queensboro Bridge, featured in
Manhattan (1979), was completed in 1909.

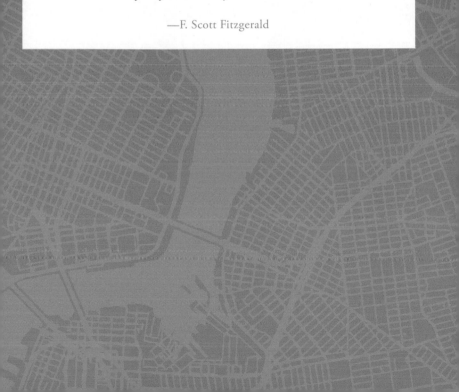

"*The city seen from the Queensboro Bridge is always the city seen for the first time, in its first wild promise of all the mystery and beauty in the world.*"

—F. Scott Fitzgerald

IF LOWER MANHATTAN IS WHERE DREAMERS
go when they're starting out, then Midtown is where they arrive once they've "made it." By the early 1900s, this part of Manhattan, stretching from Twenty-Third Street to Fifty-Ninth, was the fashionable place for anyone wealthy or famous to work and play. Most of the iconic destinations in New York City, places so full of history and shaped by stunning design so recognizable that sometimes just their silhouettes connote "New York," are located here: the world's most famous skyscrapers in the Empire State Building and Chrysler Building; the world's most famous crossroads in Times Square; the world's most famous theater district in Broadway; the world's most famous department store in Macy's; the world's most famous jewelers in Tiffany's; and the world's most famous ice-skating rink and Christmas tree at Rockefeller Center.

Hollywood may be where movies are made, but Midtown Manhattan is where movies are set. As a global capital of business, culture, and high society, Midtown has been featured in a stunning number of films, even if these locales have been re-created on sound-stages elsewhere. This area is the very definition of aspirational, where the people are as upwardly mobile in their lives and careers as the towering buildings shooting into the sky. Lower Manhattan is where people go to meet, to learn, to exchange—it's the lived-in part of Manhattan, like the parts of your home you keep hidden from houseguests. Midtown is the living room you decorate a little bit fancier than any other part of your house, the place where you'll host visitors to make an impression. The most common pastime here is simply the act of looking, and then, of course, of coveting. The reflective steel-and-glass canyons of Midtown display countless things people want, so much, in fact, you realize you can never have it all. That means there can be something a little lonely about Midtown, a little diminishing, even as all the luxury stores, glamorous theaters, and shimmering lights promise dazzle and fulfillment. And it can be frustrating here, too, especially for New Yorkers. If you work in Midtown, that mad dash walking from your subway stop to your office will invariably be interrupted by the awestruck meandering of wide-eyed tourists trying to take in everything around them and oblivious to the fact that people really do live and work here and are probably running late. Add to that aggressive taxi drivers blatantly ignoring pedestrians' right of way and you can understand the frustration of Dustin Hoffman's Ratso Rizzo at the intersection of Fifty-Eighth Street and Sixth Avenue in *Midnight Cowboy* (1969): "I'm walking here!"

But every now and then, when we take a moment to step back and reflect on the visual power of this place, longtime New Yorkers can be overcome by the beauty of Midtown, too. Just as Woody Allen and Diane Keaton are when they sit on a bench in Sutton Place Park and gaze upon the Queensboro Bridge at night in *Manhattan*. The bridge is a masterpiece, even without Gordon Willis's extraordinary black-and-white cinematography. And that bench is still there, ready for your own *Manhattan* moment—just fire up the New York Philharmonic's version of Gershwin's "Someone to Watch over Me" and the moment will be complete.

That area of the East Fifties overlooking the Queensboro Bridge, known as Sutton Place, lives up to the old cliché as "a place to see and be seen." And residents Betty Grable, Marilyn Monroe, and Lauren Bacall certainly want to be seen in *How to Marry a Millionaire* (1953). They live at 36 Sutton Place South, a modern seventeen-story apartment building built in 1949—and in its penthouse, no less, which they lease for a steal from its owner, a guy who's fled to Europe for tax evasion. The idea is that in these glamorous digs they will so dazzle New York society that each will surely hook a millionaire for a mate. Their lodgings are putting them on the right track: the high-society mansion in *My Man Godfrey* (1936) must be right nearby, given that it has a stunning view of the Queensboro Bridge and is probably located in Sutton Place.

THE WORLD'S MOST FAMOUS STREET VENT
Fifty-Second Street & Lexington Avenue, Southwest Corner

If "being seen" was her goal, Marilyn Monroe is surely one of the most seen women who's ever lived. And never was she more a subject of spectacle worth gazing upon than when her ivory skirt fluttered skyward over a New York City subway grate on the southwest corner of Fifty-Second Street and Lexington Avenue in *The Seven Year Itch* (1955). It's as iconic an image of insouciant glamour as there's ever been. And even as he was making the movie, director Billy Wilder knew it. As a stunt to promote the movie, he informed the New York press that they would be filming there. He wanted to prove that Monroe could indeed stop traffic. Well, she certainly did that.

Twentieth Century Fox costume designer William Travilla created Monroe's dress, with its flowing skirt and halter-style bodice. It's usually identified as a white dress, even though actually it's ivory. In *The Seven Year Itch*, Monroe's character wears it to see the movie *Creature from the Black Lagoon* (1954) at the Trans-Lux 52nd Street Theatre, which used to show movies there. (Imagine being that dressed up to go to the movies!) She's accompanied by the character played by Tom Ewell, and when they exit the theater she stands over a street vent . . . and the rest is history. Wilder's publicity push paid off, as not

The scene of Marilyn Monroe's skirt billowing up over the street vent in *The Seven Year Itch* had to be filmed twice: once at the actual New York City street and again on a recreation of it on a Hollywood soundstage.

only did traffic stop but two thousand people showed up to watch the filming. There were so many people, in fact, that it was impossible for Wilder to cover the moment with as many camera angles as he hoped, so he ended up restaging the scene on a Fox soundstage. The shots that appear in the movie are a combination of both the soundstage work and the location shooting.

This moment from *The Seven Year Itch* is as iconic as they come, but it's hardly singular. In fact, a similar moment occurs in a seventy-seven-second film from 1901 directed by Edwin S. Porter (of *The Great Train Robbery* fame) and George Fleming called *What Happened on Twenty-Third Street, New York City*. Walking down the street where the Hotel Chelsea is located, a woman walks over a subway grate and suddenly her skirt and petticoat balloon as well. It's a common New York City hazard: people forget that the subway is not very deep underground. It's right below street level, so to relieve the air pressure and currents swirling inside, vents open to the street surface. Walking along any New York City street with a subway beneath, you are likely to encounter these grates, and if a train speeds past, you'll certainly hear its rattle coming up from below—and you can still stand where Marilyn did today.

TIFFANY & CO.
727 Fifth Avenue

The only things that could rival Marilyn Monroe in all her eye-catching power are the glittering gems on display at Fifty-Seventh Street and Fifth Avenue, housed at America's premier jewelers, Tiffany & Co. Marilyn did sing "Diamonds Are a Girl's Best Friend," after all. And Audrey Hepburn's Holly Golightly in *Breakfast at Tiffany's* (1961) certainly agrees. At the start of the film we see her starting the day—or, more likely, ending it after a very long night—walking toward the store windows with a coffee in hand and a paper bag, sunglasses draping her eyes and chicly outfitted in a black dress by Givenchy. Holly gazes on a few of the shiny trinkets within, while slowly eating a danish pastry. Forty years later, Patrick Dempsey would propose to

Tiffany & Co.'s headquarters, where Audrey Hepburn eats a quick meal—and has a feast for the eyes—at the beginning of *Breakfast at Tiffany's*, has stood at its Fifth Avenue location since 1906.

Reese Witherspoon at the beginning of *Sweet Home Alabama* (2002) in the expansive showroom of Tiffany's.

And one imagines this is where Barbara Stanwyck's Lee Leander steals a bracelet before scurrying to a nearby pawnshop to unload it at the beginning of *Remember the Night* (1940). She's caught in the act of selling it, but her lawyer's defense at her trial—that she's been hypnotized by the gems—is one for the ages: "The bracelet is under a powerful light. The young girl stares at it, closer, closer. The great central stone flashes blindingly in her eyes—blue, green, purple, orange! Closer, still closer!" The message is clear: people are drawn to the baubles of Fifth Avenue jewelry stores, and Tiffany's is the grandest, like a moth to flame. On a sadder note, it's at Tiffany's where Jon Voight's Joe in *Midnight Cowboy* (1969) sees a homeless man passed out on the sidewalk, with passersby literally stepping over him. That's the nature of New York City, and particularly Midtown: it's a place of superlatives, where extreme wealth and extreme poverty can coexist just footsteps from each other.

FAO SCHWARZ
30 Rockefeller Plaza (currently)

While we're on the subject of coveting, Fifty-Eighth Street and Fifth Avenue was the location of the world's most famous repository of toys beyond Santa's Workshop from 1931 to 2015. That location of FAO Schwarz was arguably the most beloved toy store of all time. In the film *Big* (1988), it was where Tom Hanks and Robert Loggia played "Heart & Soul" and "Chopsticks" with their feet upon the keys of a giant floor-length piano. The interiors of FAO Schwarz were also used as a stand-in for the interiors of Duncan's Toy Chest, the store "Wet Bandits" Joe Pesci and Daniel Stern plan to rob on Christmas Eve in *Home Alone 2: Lost in New York*. In the film, the owner of Duncan's Toy Chest is played by Eddie Bracken, a popular Hollywood star of the 1940s, perhaps best known for his hilarious turn in another Christmas movie, Preston Sturges's *The Miracle of Morgan's Creek* (1944). Sadly, FAO Schwarz closed in 2015—it had been purchased by Toys "R" Us, which suffered its own financial collapse. However, a new version of FAO Schwarz opened at 30 Rockefeller Plaza in late 2018.

The foot-operated electronic keyboard was first installed at FAO Schwarz in 1982, but director Penny Marshall had an entirely new one built just for the filming of *Big*.

Where to Eat:
21 Club

All that shopping on Fifth Avenue can work up quite an appetite. Why not sate yourself at 21 Club, where countless movie stars have dined? Elizabeth Taylor, Marilyn Monroe, Sammy Davis Jr., Judy Garland, Gloria Swanson, and Mae West were such regular patrons they even had their own private wine collections stored at 21. Yes, that whiff of something potent you smell isn't just the delicious food, it's the smell of power. So of course 21 Club (the name comes from its address, 21 West Fifty-Second Street) was featured in *Wall Street* (1987), and it was the preferred haunt of Burt Lancaster's tyrannical gossip columnist J. J. Hunsecker in *Sweet Smell of Success* (1957). In the film, Hunsecker holds court from a table with his back to the wall, entertaining celebrities and politicians whose reputations he could elevate or destroy with a *rap-tap-tap* of his typewriter. Hunsecker even has the 21 management keep a telephone on

21 Club's main dining room is dimly lit with dark wood, checkered table cloths, and model airplanes hanging from the ceiling—the perfect lair for J. J. Hunsecker to rule New York in *Sweet Smell of Success*, starring Tony Curtis and Burt Lancaster.

21 opened at its location on Fifty-Second Street between Sixth and Fifth Avenues in 1929 and functioned as a speakeasy during Prohibition.

his table, just in case he needs to call in a scoop at any moment. Many jazz clubs were located on Fifty-Second Street from the 1930s through the '50s—street signs still mark its honorary name, "Swing Street." In *The Lost Weekend* (1945), Ray Milland's alcoholic Don Birnam steals a purse at one of these clubs, the fictional Harry & Joe's, which is listed as being at 13 West Fifty-Second Street and, thus, presumably right next door to the 21 Club.

And 21 is the last of these Fifty-Second Street nightclubs from the era of *The Lost Weekend* to survive. It remains the very definition of refinement and luxury—so gentlemen, take note: jackets are required. The only gentleman who didn't have to worry about that was L. B. Jefferies in *Rear Window*. Laid up with his broken leg, Jefferies was treated in his apartment to a catered dinner from 21 by his girlfriend, Lisa. Lisa and Jeff love each other, but they're coming from very different places in life and in the city. Jeff is Greenwich Village through and through, unpretentious and used to roughing it; Lisa is all Midtown refinement, as epitomized by her choice of 21 for his celebratory dinner.

Where to Eat:
Russian Tea Room

The same year 21 Club moved to its current home, the Russian Tea Room moved to its own. Located since 1929 at 150 West Fifty-Seventh Street, this fine dining establishment was founded by former members of the Imperial Russian Ballet, all emigrés in New York City following the Bolshevik Revolution of 1917. It's been closed at various points over the decades and gone through redecorations, but the red leather half-circle booths, green walls, gilded accents, and Imperial Russian eagle motifs have been pretty much constants. Like 21 Club, it's featured in *Sweet Smell of Success*, but its most famous starring role might be in Sydney Pollack's *Tootsie* (1982), in which the director plays hardened agent George Fields, who's initially taken in by his client Michael Dorsey's scheme to make it as an actor by auditioning for parts as a woman. At the Russian Tea Room, Michael reveals to his agent the truth behind his scheme and Pollack's George replies with one of the best deadpan lines in the movie: "Michael, I begged you to get some therapy."

Dorothy Michaels (Dustin Hoffman) reveals to agent George Fields (Sydney Pollack) that he's really Michael Dorsey, an actor he represents, over drinks at the Russian Tea Room in *Tootsie*.

NIGHTCLUB NIRVANA

The proliferation of radio in the 1920s helped raise the profile of individual bands and orchestras—not to mention crooners—in a way that simply had not been possible before. But the real money for musicians was still in performing live, and starting in the late '20s and continuing through the 1950s, Midtown was boomtown for nightclubs. Often, radio broadcasts of orchestras took place live at nightclubs to give listeners a vicarious sense of glamour. For anyone coveting glitz and sophistication, the Stork Club on Fifty-Eighth Street, was the place to be. From 1929 to 1965 it hosted movie stars, ex-presidents, royalty—basically anyone who was famous.

In *All About Eve* (1950), it's the club where Margo (Bette Davis) and Bill (Gary Merrill) announce their engagement. And it's where Henry Fonda's jazz musician plays in *The Wrong Man* (1956), until he's accused of a robbery he clearly had not committed—to the club owner's credit, we see him still playing at the club even after his legal difficulties begin.

The Wrong Man dramatized a true story, about a Stork Club musician named Manny Balestrero (Henry Fonda) unjustly accused of a crime he didn't commit.

The nightclub lent its name to a 1945 movie. *The Stork Club* starred Betty Hutton as a coat-check girl who longs for the return of her musician boyfriend who's off fighting in World War II.

Club Carousel was a noted jazz club on Fifty-Second Street—Rosemary Clooney's Betty in *White Christmas* (1954), having left in a fit of anger and misunderstanding the cozy act she had helped create up in Vermont, performs at the Carousel Club, its name slightly changed, as a solo act. Wearing a slinky black dress, and surrounded by a posse of backup dancers (including a young, uncredited George Chakiris of later *West Side Story* fame), she sings the bluesy Irving Berlin lament "Love, You Didn't Do Right by Me." Not far away, on Broadway between Fifty-Second and Fifty-Third Streets, was the original Birdland jazz club, named after its most famous headliner Charlie "Yardbird" Parker. A club with that name survives, but in a different location, Forty-Fourth Street between Eighth and Ninth Avenues. The original was depicted in Clint Eastwood's Charlie Parker biopic, *Bird* (1988). And at El Morocco, originally located at 154 East Fifty-Fourth Street, Barbra Streisand's Katie first encounters Robert Redford's Hubbell (who's fallen asleep at the bar) in *The Way We Were* (1973)—after the period in which that scene is set, the real-life El Morocco would move farther east on Fifty-Fourth Street, where it would remain until closing in 1997.

Club Carousel was recreated on a soundstage for *White Christmas (co-star Rosemary Clooney is seen here)*. The real location was at 66 West Fifty-Second Street.

Where to Drink:

Jimmy's Corner

For a less posh entertainment venue, head to Forty-Fourth Street dive bar Jimmy's Corner, between Sixth and Seventh Avenues. This is where Martin Scorsese filmed the last scene of *Raging Bull* (1980), in which Robert De Niro's Jake LaMotta preps for the stand-up act he was known to perform in his later years, when he transitioned from boxing to entertainment. LaMotta would crack jokes, give interpretive readings of Shakespeare, Paddy Chayefsky, and Rod Serling, and put the moves on ladies in attendance. LaMotta died in 2017 at age ninety-five, having been married a little over four years to his seventh wife, who, based on what we saw of LaMotta in the film, was a very brave woman.

Where to Drink:

The Rainbow Room

On the sixty-fifth floor of 30 Rockefeller Plaza sits the Rainbow Room, one of the most sophisticated and elegant event spaces in the history of New York. Opened in 1934, the Rainbow Room was decorated in part by Vincente Minnelli before he moved to Hollywood to become one of the most celebrated directors in history. He chose the shade of plum that would be the color of the Rainbow Room's walls and featured as an accent on other furnishings throughout. Bill Pullman's Walter takes Meg Ryan's Annie to the Rainbow Room for dinner in *Sleepless in Seattle* (1993). Their table has a killer view of the Empire State Building and when a heart appears on the side of the skyscraper, she knows she has to leave Walter behind and go there to find her true love, Tom Hanks's Sam. Today, the restaurant portion of the Rainbow Room is only available to reserve for private events, but there is a bar open to the public called Bar Sixty-Five, which includes the highest terrace on which drinks are served in Manhattan. It's become a popular New Year's Eve destination, with tickets going for a paltry $325 per person as of 2018.

ROCKEFELLER CENTER
30 Rockefeller Plaza

This campus of towering office skyscrapers, first proposed by oil tycoon John D. Rockefeller Jr., as a sprawling urban renewal project for Midtown in the late 1920s, comprises nineteen buildings from Forty-Eighth Street to Fifty-First Street, but it all started with 30 Rockefeller Plaza, which broke ground in 1930. Lovingly nicknamed 30 Rock (the site and namesake of Tina Fey's comedy series), it was originally known as the RCA Building, as Rockefeller had entered into an agreement with the Radio Corporation of America to cofinance the property. RCA owned the radio network NBC, which, after expanding into television and other media, still has its headquarters in 30 Rock today. *Desk Set* (1957), the charming, confectionary second-to-last onscreen pairing of Katharine Hepburn and Spencer Tracy, takes place at a TV network obviously meant to serve as a stand-in for NBC, with offices that deliberately evoke 30 Rock—director Walter Lang actually did film the exterior of the RCA Building to serve as the exterior of the building where Hepburn's network TV researcher works.

Many other buildings in Rockefeller Center followed the construction of the RCA Building, some much later, like the Time-Life

Spencer Tracy and Katharine Hepburn share a chilly lunch on a windswept terrace of a building meant to be 30 Rock in *Desk Set*.

Katharine Hepburn's Bunny Watson works at the fictional Federal Broadcasting Network as a researcher—someone who fact-checks broadcasts for accuracy in advance of airing.

Building in 1959, where the ad agency of Jon Hamm's Don Draper was located in the later seasons of *Mad Men*. But on the Fifth Avenue–facing side of 30 Rock, overlooking the ice rink where Buddy (Will Ferrell) and Jovie (Zooey Deschanel) skate in *Elf* (2003), settled into a concourse of shops and restaurants that sits below the RCA Building, is the location of the Rockefeller Center Christmas Tree, which, for every year since the tradition began in 1933, has been the most famous Christmas tree in the world. A different tree each year, almost always a Norway spruce, is cut down from somewhere across the United States (though a tree from Ontario was once selected) and donated to the site. The selection process involves looking for a tree that's between seventy-four and ninety-four feet tall, though some throughout its history have been shorter or taller. It's in front of the Rockefeller Center Christmas Tree of 1991 that director Chris Columbus filmed the reunion of Kevin McCallister (Macaulay Culkin) and his mother (Catherine O'Hara) in *Home Alone 2: Lost in New York*.

Keep walking east from the ice rink until you reach Fifth Avenue. On this side of Rockefeller Center you'll find Lee Lawrie's statue of Atlas, cast in bronze and installed here in 1937. In the opening scene of Elia Kazan's *Gentleman's Agreement* (1947) Gregory Peck's journalist Philip Schuyler Green takes his ten-year-old son, Tommy (Dean Stockwell), to see it. Tommy says to his dad that his grandmother always says that he, a widowed father, is just like Atlas, carrying the world on his shoulders.

RADIO CITY MUSIC HALL
1260 Sixth Avenue

Reflecting the Radio Corporation of America's history as a founder of Rockefeller Center is Radio City Music Hall, opened to the public in 1932 and as much an art deco playground for musical acts and stage shows today as it was back then. Many Tony and Grammy Awards broadcasts have been held here, and it's the home of the legendary *Radio City Christmas Spectacular*, with its high-kicking chorus line, the Radio City Rockettes. Radio City Music Hall's nearly six-thousand-seat auditorium made it the world's largest in 1932, and what's extraordinary is that movies were frequently shown here in addition to live performances. It was an experience much like what Joe, the narrator of *Radio Days* (1987), describes when he saw a movie there in the 1940s: the first thing you see upon entering Radio City Music Hall is its grand staircase nestled against a red wall accented with abstract gilded clouds. Joe says that climbing those stairs up to the mezzanine or balcony felt like ascending to heaven. Not to come crashing down from that golden childhood reverie, but inside the auditorium itself, as a movie is playing, is also where Norman Lloyd's villain, Fry, shoots at his pursuers in *Saboteur*, causing a panic.

THE NEW YORK PUBLIC LIBRARY
476 Fifth Avenue (Main Branch)

After catching a musical act at Radio City Music Hall, maybe you want to rest your ears a bit—those acoustics are second to none. So why not enjoy the quiet of the New York Public Library on the eastern edge of Bryant Park? Opened to the public in 1911, this is one of the largest libraries in the world, containing over 2.5 million volumes on its shelves. You can't miss the imposing sculpted lions that flank the massive stairs leading up from Fifth Avenue to the entrance; they're called Patience and Fortitude, good qualities for any scholar visiting the library to have. But the peace and quiet at the New York Public Library was rudely interrupted by a restless specter in *Ghostbusters* (1984), with books flying off the shelves. It's enough to drive a book lover to distraction! On a less supernatural but equally tumultuous note, the staircase inside the New York Public Library is where in *Network* (1976) Peter Finch's Howard Beale is escorted, ranting, to meet with Ned Beatty's network executive who hopes to coopt the anchor's performatively angry ramblings to further his corporate agenda. The library here was meant to stand in as the lobby of an office building. Be sure to visit the Main Reading Room on the third floor, check out the rotating exhibition featured downstairs and then enjoy, if it's seasonable, sitting outside in Bryant Park. On Monday nights during the summer, classic films are projected on a giant screen that looms over the park's main lawn, where cinephiles stretch blankets over the grass to catch films like *Key Largo* (1948) and *Desk Set*.

THE EMPIRE STATE BUILDING
20 West Thirty-Fourth Street

It's hard to believe but the Empire State Building—1,250 feet tall with a 204-foot antenna and for many decades the tallest building in the world—took only fourteen months to build. Finished in May 1931, its builders had "topped out" its superstructure after completing an average of four-and-a-half floors per week. Its most famous cinematic depiction, one so crucial to the skyscraper's place in our collective memory, *King Kong* (1933), made its debut in New York City just

Leo McCarey's *Love Affair* (1939), starring Irene Dunne and Charles Boyer, was remade twice—by McCarey himself in 1957 as *An Affair to Remember*, and again as *Love Affair* in 1994, starring Warren Beatty and his real-life wife Annette Bening.

twenty-two months later. At the end of the film, Kong climbs to the top of the Empire State Building. Note, the building didn't yet have its antenna spire, just a rounded top that was intended to be a dock for dirigibles (though only one such airship ever docked, and only for three minutes, because it was dangerous). Kong clings to the outside of what would become the enclosed 102nd-floor observation deck, Ann Darrow (Fay Wray) clutched in one hand and swatting attacking planes with the other. Kong is ultimately felled by the airplanes' machine guns and falls 1,250 feet to the ground.

More hopeful romances have centered around the Empire State Building as well, even if these sometimes have a whiff of tragedy around them, too. Charles Boyer's Michel Marnay falls in love with Irene Dunne's Terry McKay aboard an ocean liner in *Love Affair* (1939). They agree to part for six months to settle up loose ends, then meet again at the top of the Empire State Building. In this version of the story, Marnay waits for McKay in the enclosed observation area on the 102nd floor. While she's walking to the Empire State Building, she keeps her eyes on the building and not the street—and is hit by a car. She survives, but is never able to send word to Marnay, who, after hours of waiting, finally leaves, heartbroken. And she may never be able to walk again. Fearful of his reaction to her potential handicap, she never reaches out to him. Remember, though, this is a hopeful romance! So we'll say no more, in case you haven't seen it.

If you've never watched *Love Affair*, the odds are better you've seen its remake, also helmed by the original film's director, Leo McCarey, *An Affair*

An Affair to Remember features one of Cary Grant's most romantic roles, but the film itself is also a sharp media satire, particularly of the dehumanizing power of the tabloid press.

An instrumental version of the theme from *An Affair to Remember*, "Our Love Affair," appears on the soundtrack at various points of *Sleepless in Seattle*.

to Remember (1957). Cary Grant and Deborah Kerr step into the roles played by Boyer and Dunne, though Grant's character has been renamed Nickie Ferrante.

It's on the open-air eighty-sixth-floor observation deck, however, where Meg Ryan's Annie goes to meet Tom Hanks's Sam at the end of *Sleepless in Seattle*, a movie constructed in part as an homage to *An Affair to Remember*.

In reality, a heart does not appear on the side of the Empire State Building on Valentine's Day the way it's depicted in *Sleepless in Seattle*, but the top floors and spire are illuminated red for the holiday.

THE "OLD" PENN STATION

Today, there's a lot of interest in preserving the past, particularly when it comes to architectural treasures. But that's a relatively recent phenomenon, as the case of the old Penn Station proves. Opened to the public in 1910, and named after the Pennsylvania Railroad, the company whose interstate trains would enter the station, it was a jewel. The main waiting room was 314 feet long, 108 feet wide, and 150 feet high, rivaling the scale of the nave of St. Peter's Basilica in Rome, and its facade was in the Greco-Roman style, adorned with Doric columns. Capable from the beginning of facilitating the arrival of over one thousand trains per day, Penn Station was a departure point for those looking to leave the state and also travel to Long Island. During World War II, countless servicemen and women streamed through here as shown in Vincente Minnelli's *The Clock* (1945). Gregory Peck

You can get a sense of the scale of the original Penn Station in Vincente Minnelli's *The Clock*, where Robert Walker's Joe first meets Judy Garland's Alice—and where they find each other again after they're separated later in the film.

and Ingrid Bergman board a train from Penn Station in *Spellbound* (1945) on their journey to break through his amnesia and clear him of a murder charge. Joel McCrea chases after his wife (Claudette Colbert) at Penn Station in *The Palm Beach Story* (1942) after she decides to run away and divorce him so she can marry a millionaire who can provide her husband the financial support she feels he deserves.

Only the underground concourse of the original Penn Station remains, completely remodeled. The classical superstructure that stretched from Thirty-First to Thirty-Third Street and between Seventh and Eighth Avenues, occupying eight acres, was torn down in 1963 after the company sold the "air rights" above the underground rail tracks to developers who planned and built the current Madison Square Garden where the beautiful terminal once sat. When the old Penn Station was torn down, *New York Times* architectural critic Ada Louise Huxtable wrote, "The tragedy is that our own times not only could not produce such a building, but cannot even maintain it." The outcry was so severe that the movement to preserve historic architecture in the United States was given a higher profile than ever before. But the current, completely underground version of Penn Station that took its place is still packed with commuters who board Long Island Railroad, Amtrak, and New Jersey Transit trains at all hours of the day—much like Bruno Antony (Robert Walker) and Guy Haines (Farley Granger) do in *Strangers on a Train* (1951). When they arrive at Penn Station, Alfred Hitchcock's camera is trained solely at their feet, and the men separately board the train where they are fated to meet.

MACY'S
151 West Thirty-Fourth Street

Macy's moved to its present location at Thirty-Fourth Street and Herald Square in 1902, and, in the years after, the retail powerhouse bought up the rest of its block so that it stretches all the way from Sixth Avenue to Seventh. Just three years after the move came the first film to be shot at the Macy's Herald Square location. Edwin S. Porter's *The Kleptomaniac* (1905) contrasts what happens when a well-dressed, wealthy-looking woman steals several items at Macy's with an obviously impoverished mother stealing a loaf of bread at another store—both women end up at court to await justice, but the law separates the poor mother from her child and imprisons her, a heartbreaking scene, while the rich woman is released with naught but a warning. *The Kleptomaniac* is the first film featuring Macy's,

Edmund Gwenn's Kris Kringle presides over the end of the Macy's Thanksgiving Day Parade where it wraps up on the Thirty-Fourth Street side of the store in *Miracle on 34th Street*.

British actor Edmund Gwenn won the Best Supporting Actor Oscar for his work in *Miracle on 34th Street*—he'd been acting for fifty-two years at that point, though he was probably best known in the United States for having played a hitman in Alfred Hitchcock's *Foreign Correspondent*.

but the first film shot on location in New York altogether was filmed right outside on Herald Square (before Macy's was built). It's simply called *Herald Square* and it was just a documentary street scene shot by Edison cameraman William Heise on May 11, 1896. What's old is new again: the long-since expired copyrights on turn-of-the-twentieth-century Edison films, along with the fact that they are so very short, means that you can find most of them online, including both *Herald Square* and *The Kleptomaniac*.

Macy's Thanksgiving Day Parade began in 1924, and twenty-three years later it was a crucial plot point at the beginning of *Miracle on 34th Street* (1947). When Macy's event planner Doris Walker (Maureen O'Hara) discovers that the Santa Claus the store had hired to appear in the parade is drunk, she hires a worthy replacement (Edmund Gwenn) who just happens to be named Kris Kringle. He stays on to be the Santa kids visit in the store, and causes an uproar when he starts recommending customers visit rival retailers for items Macy's doesn't have in stock. Company head R. H. Macy ends up embracing Kringle's approach as a goodwill marketing stunt, which is good news since everyone in the movie has been fretting about what "Mr. Macy" will think. In real life, R. H. Macy had died seventy years earlier and the Macy family had divested itself of any ownership of the company by 1895, selling it to brothers Isidor and Nathan Straus. Isidor Straus famously died along with his wife on board the *Titanic*, leaving his brother Nathan to steer Macy's future. But why worry about historical accuracy when you can have an actual Mr. Macy running the store?

BELLEVUE HOSPITAL
462 First Avenue

If you head east down Twenty-Eighth Street all the way to the East River you'll run into Bellevue Hospital, where Porter Hall's psychiatrist character has Kris Kringle committed for supposedly being mentally ill. Since 1879, Bellevue has been a world leader in mental health treatment with "Bellevue" often standing in as a term that implies psychiatric care. Kringle deliberately fails his psychological evaluation at Bellevue, setting off the court case that seeks to determine whether or not he really is Santa Claus. In *The Lost Weekend*, Ray Milland's Don Birnam wakes up from a drunken stupor in the alcoholics ward at Bellevue. Despite desperately needing treatment, he escapes from the hospital when another patient is making a commotion. Founded in 1736, Bellevue is the oldest public hospital in the United States still in operation, and *The Lost Weekend* is the only time a film production has been allowed to film on-site. The alcoholics ward you see in the film is the actual alcoholics ward in the hospital itself.

THE WALDORF-ASTORIA
301 Park Avenue

A skyscraper hotel like nothing before it, the Waldorf-Astoria helped redefine the hospitality industry in the midtwentieth century by showing that efficiency and luxury could be combined. By any standard a glamorous, desirable place to stay—Frank Sinatra maintained a suite at the Waldorf-Astoria from 1979 to 1988—the hotel projected a sense of refinement and personal attention on a huge scale: it's a forty-seven-story building, and, until 1963 and the opening of the Hotel Ukraina in Moscow, was the tallest hotel in the world. The Waldorf-Astoria is essentially the Empire State Building of hotels, and the comparison isn't just because they're both beautiful works of art deco architecture and became symbols of New York after they both opened in 1931.

Their building histories are intertwined: the original Waldorf-Astoria took up much of the block from Thirty-Third Street to Thirty-Fourth Street on Fifth Avenue. It sat on the site where the Empire State Building would be built. The hyphenated name alludes to the fact that it was a hybrid—two separate hotels were built right next to each other on the same block by feuding members of the Astor family. The first, the Waldorf Hotel, was built in 1893 and the second, the Astoria, came in 1897. Eventually, they merged. By the late 1920s, it made sense to move the hotel farther north in Midtown to the more fashionable address of Fiftieth Street and Park Avenue, making way for the Empire State Building project—and allowing for the Waldorf-Astoria to become an art deco skyscraper that would be the toast of the city. When *Grand Hotel* was remade in 1945 with a New York City setting, the hotel at its center had to be the Waldorf. The resulting film, *Week-End at the Waldorf*, keeps some of the plot threads of the original book and movie but with a few updated twists.

Unfortunately, the owners of the Waldorf-Astoria closed it in 2017 for a refurbishment intended to turn the building into a luxury apartment complex with only a few astronomically pricy hotel rooms available for short stays. But visiting it had always been a transporting experience: you walk in through the Park Avenue entrance and go up a

Week-End at the Waldorf was a new adaptation of *Grand Hotel* that transplanted the action from Berlin to New York's Waldorf-Astoria. It starred Van Johnson, Ginger Rogers, Lana Turner, Walter Pidgeon, and Edward Arnold.

flight of marble stairs until you reach a landing that leads to the dark, wood-paneled lobby, with four large rectangular wood pillars accented with concentric gold lines. Director Wes Anderson filmed here with the intention of the Waldorf-Astoria's lobby serving as the lobby of the Lindbergh Palace Hotel, where Gene Hackman's patriarch lives in *The Royal Tenenbaums* (2001). The year of that film's release, 2001, was a big one for the Waldorf-Astoria, because some critical scenes in the delightful romantic comedy *Serendipity* were set there. Most importantly, it's where Kate Beckinsale's Sara engages in a bet with John Cusack's Jonathan—they are to get in separate elevators and each pick, without telling the other, a floor on which to exit. If both get off on the same floor, that means they're meant to be together. If they don't, well, that's that.

THE PLAZA HOTEL
768 Fifth Avenue

More so even than the Waldorf-Astoria, the Plaza is the most famous hotel in New York City. It's an icon of luxury and taste that's been emulated countless times by other hotels around the world that have adopted the name "Plaza," as well, to try to capture a little of the glamour of this Fifth Avenue original. This nineteen-floor French château-style urban palace, located right across the southeast corner of Central Park was already so instantly identifiable with New York's upper crust that F. Scott Fitzgerald wrote it into *The Great Gatsby* in 1925. It's where Tom and Daisy Buchanan, sweltering from the Long Island summer heat and their own emotional turmoil, want to go to cool off. As depicted in Baz Luhrmann's 2013 film version of the novel, they take up residence in a suite and order a large block of ice sent up to them, which a butler chisels away with the satisfying *thunk-thunk-thunk* of an ice pick.

The most famous resident of the Plaza has to be a fictional little girl: Eloise, the mischievous six-year-old who starred in a series of children's books, starting with *Eloise: A Book for Precocious Grown-Ups*, written by Kay Thompson and illustrated by Hilary Knight. Eloise lives on the "tippy-top" floor of the hotel with her pug, Weenie, and

Barbra Streisand's Katie sees her ex-husband Hubbell (Robert Redford) one last time in front of the Plaza Hotel at the end of *The Way We Were*.

turtle, Skipperdee. Visit the Plaza and on a hallway on the south edge of the airy and bustling Palm Court restaurant you'll find a life-size portrait of Eloise. Her creator Thompson was a mover-and-shaker in New York and Hollywood. She appears as a fashion magazine editor, though really playing a version of herself, in Stanley Donen's *Funny Face* (1957), where her mantra is "think pink." It's unclear who, if anyone, inspired Thompson to create Eloise, but it's been suggested she may have based the look of the spunky tyke on her real-life goddaughter, Liza Minnelli.

Another precocious child checked in to the Plaza using his father's credit card: Kevin McCallister in *Home Alone 2: Lost in New York*. Trust me, at no point have the hotel staff ever been as villainously intrusive as Tim Curry's concierge and Rob Schneider's bellhop in the film. Having boarded the wrong flight by mistake, Kevin, in possession of his father's bag, including his dad's credit cards, knows there's only one place to stay: the Plaza, because he saw it on TV. He followed in the footsteps of Paul Hogan's Mick Dundee, who stayed at the Plaza after being brought to New York by the *Newsday* reporter whose life he saved, in *Crocodile Dundee* (1986). Mick finds himself confused by the purpose of the bidet in his suite. In *Almost Famous* (2000), teenage Rolling Stone reporter William Miller (Patrick Fugit) follows rock 'n' roll fanatic Penny Lane (Kate Hudson) to the Plaza. It's also here where Jeff Bridges's Jack receives a Pinocchio doll from a small child that he keeps with him throughout *The Fisher King* (1991). And it was at the Plaza's Oak Room where Rooney Mara's Therese reunites with Cate Blanchett's Carol at the end of the Todd Haynes 1950s-set film *Carol* (2015).

Spotlight on North by Northwest (1959)

The Plaza Hotel has always been a magnet for celebrities and routinely a setting in films, but it's never had a greater starring role than in Alfred Hitchcock's "wrong man on the run" film from 1959. Cary Grant was a frequent guest at the Plaza and he stayed there throughout the duration of the shoot—but the hotel itself is an important part of the plot.

Ad man Thornhill takes a meeting at the Plaza's swanky Oak Bar. When he realizes he needs to send a message to his mother, he signals for a waiter—who just happened to be paging spy George Kaplan at the moment. Kaplan's evil pursuers thus think Thornhill is Kaplan and they kidnap him right as he's exiting the bar.

After he eludes his kidnappers, Thornhill returns to the Plaza the next day to piece together how this case of mistaken identity happened. He and his mother gain access to the room of the spy Kaplan, whose clothes are still hanging in the closet. "Well, obviously, they've mistaken me for a much shorter man," Thornhill says, holding up Kaplan's trousers.

Thornhill and his mother enter a crowded elevator after finishing combing through Kaplan's hotel room—and he notices that the men who kidnapped him are there. Not believing him to be in any real danger, Thornhill's mother quips, "You gentlemen aren't really trying to kill my son, are you?"

THE UNITED NATIONS BUILDING
405 East Forty-Second Street

The United Nations Building, set in the midst of a whole complex of related structures stretching from Forty-Second Street to Forty-Eighth Street on the East River, was completed in 1952. Standing thirty-nine floors, this rectangular glass-and-steel building is flanked by rows of flags representing the organization's many member nations. In *North by Northwest*, Cary Grant's Roger Thornhill heads here to find Lester

Though many films included scenes set at the United Nations Building, from *North by Northwest* to *Live and Let Die* (1973), no film production was allowed to shoot on location at the site until Sydney Pollack's *The Interpreter*, released in 2005.

Townsend, the man who he thought had kidnapped him and had him taken to his estate on Long Island. When Townsend is presented to him—after apparently addressing the General Assembly—Thornhill realizes this is not the man who had absconded with him. Right as he asks Townsend, "Well, then, who are those people living in your house?" Townsend's face jolts to an expression of shock and he collapses, a knife having been thrown into his back. Thornhill, trying to help him, pulls the knife out of his back, which, to all present, appears like he's the one who killed Townsend. Now he has to go on the run.

GRAND CENTRAL TERMINAL
89 East Forty-Second Street

When Grand Central Terminal opened in 1913, it set a new standard for train stations the world over. It wasn't just a place for departures and arrivals, for passengers to hurry through and waiting families to bide their time before loved ones arrive. It was a work of art unto itself, with a lustrous depiction of the night sky's constellations embedded into its concave ceiling, and a massive four-sided clock with opal faces that Christie's has valued at a minimum of $10 million. The staircases that flank either side of the main concourse are made of marble, as are the vaulted arches that lead to the sixty-seven train tracks at the site. It's so beautiful that *Travel + Leisure* magazine reported 21.9 million visitors came to the station just to tour it in 2013—that's on top of the almost 70 million commuters who pass through each year. Cary Grant's Roger Thornhill in *North by Northwest*, wearing sunglasses and maybe trying a little too hard to be inconspicuous, was one of those who bought a train ticket here to escape the city after he became a wanted man. (You can stand exactly where he stood if you go to ticket window #6.) It's also where a shootout occurs in *Carlito's Way* (1993), and a lavish boardroom at Grand Central Terminal, built for directors of the railroads, served as the room where the Five Families confer when they were trying to end open bloodshed in *The Godfather*. The exterior of that building where the meeting is held is shown to be the exterior of the Federal Reserve Bank downtown, however.

Grand Central Terminal, known by New Yorkers more informally
as Grand Central Station, is also where Gene Hackman's Lex
Luthor has his lair in *Superman: The Movie*. If hiding in plain sight
is the best approach when avoiding the law, then making your
hideout the abandoned space under one of the world's most visited
tourist attractions has to be foolproof, right?

Ned Beatty plays Otis, a
bumbling henchman of Lex
Luthor, who approaches
the hideout via the main
concourse, then descends
down to a subway track, where
there's a secret door to the lair.

Valerie Perrine's henchwoman, Eve
Teschmacher, lives in this converted
underground space, which has been
made quite luxurious: a swimming
pool is here, accented by the
marble arches you can see up in
the concourse proper. Luthor has
installed computers to monitor his
evil schemes.

Superman and Lex
Luthor technically live
in the city of Metropolis,
which in the universe of
Superman: The Movie
must just be a nickname
for New York City,
given the presence of
Grand Central Terminal,
the Statue of Liberty,
and other Big Apple
locations.

TIMES SQUARE

It's a canyon of neon signs and LED billboards like no other, an elec-
trified playland of theaters, and storefronts, street hawkers, and novel-
ty acts that'll give your optic nerves a workout—and try your patience
from the sheer number of people packed into it, gazing at everything.
You can see how overwhelmed and panicked Michael Keaton's Riggan
Thomson in *Birdman* (2013) would be when, during a production of
the play *What We Talk About When We Talk About Love* he's starring in
at the St. James Theatre on Forty-Fourth Street, he's locked out from
the stage wearing only his underwear. In order for the play to resume
has to leave the theater altogether via the back entrance, make his way
through the teeming throngs of Times Square, and reenter the theater
from the front. Several blocks north, you can imagine the sense of
power Burt Lancaster's dictatorial gossip columnist J. J. Hunsecker in
Sweet Smell of Success feels as he stands on the balcony of his apartment
overlooking Times Square in the Brill Building at 1619 Broadway. The
script of Alexander Mackendrick's film is too subtle to include such
a line, but standing high above, lording over Times Square, you can
almost hear Hunsecker saying, "I rule this town."

Michael Keaton's Riggan Thomson feels exposed in Times Square
in *Birdman* (2014).

It was at the Liberty Theatre on Forty-Second Street, now a rental space, where Cohan starred in *Little Johnny Jones*, the show that introduced to America the song "Yankee Doodle Boy."

The term "seeing the sights" seems like it was invented for Times Square. No sight is seen more than the illuminated crystal ball that descends down a pole from the building One Times Square at the crossroad's southern terminus. And Times Square is a crossroads, the intersection of Broadway and Seventh Avenue that stretches from Forty-Second Street to Forty-Seventh. Right in the center you can find the statue of George M. Cohan, the composer and performer who wrote "You're a Grand Old Flag," "Over There," and "Give My Regards to Broadway," and was played by James Cagney in the Michael Curtiz biopic *Yankee Doodle Dandy* (1942).

When Cohan debuted his first show on Broadway in 1901, Times Square was known under a different name. It was Longacre Square, but even then it looked like a glittering metropolis and a far cry from the way it was depicted in Buster Keaton and John Blystone's *Our Hospitality* in 1923. That silent comedy, set one hundred years earlier in the 1820s, includes a joke upfront about the intersection of Broadway and Forty-Second

Prince Edward (James Marsden) pops into Times Square. The New York City sewer is a portal to another world in *Enchanted.*

Street then being too crowded, even though it's depicted as empty farmland. Longacre Square was renamed Times Square in 1904, with the blessing of Mayor George McClellan Jr., to commemorate the *New York Times* moving its office there. The paper's owner, Adolph Ochs, came up with the tradition of the New Year's Eve ball drop in 1908. The globe descended on the rooftop of One Times Square, then the *New York Times* office building, and it's been held there ever since, with well over 100,000 people attending the celebration each December 31. This is a place for people to come together. Think of how a sewer manhole cover in the middle of Times Square is a portal to the animated realm of Andalasia in *Enchanted* (2007), and from where Giselle (Amy Adams) and her beau Prince Edward (James Marsden) first pop up to experience New York. Times Square is also the first thing super-soldier Steve Rogers sees when he wakes up in the twenty-first century in *Captain America: The First Avenger* (2011)—he knows right away he's not in the 1940s anymore.

Where to Eat:

Sardi's

Sardi's was founded by an Italian immigrant couple in 1921 on the site of what would become the St. James Theatre. When construction was set to begin, the Shubert brothers, the impresarios who owned many Broadway theaters (the present version of their company, the Shubert Organization still owns and manages a huge number of Broadway venues today), moved Sardi's farther down Forty-Fourth Street, where it's been located ever since 1927. The first thing you'll see upon entering are the hundreds of caricatures of celebrities on the walls. This was a tradition begun early on by a friend of the Sardis, Alex Gard, a Russian immigrant, who agreed to create one caricature for them a day in exchange for a meal. Others took up the mantle after Gard died in 1948. Pass by the windows of Sardi's on Forty-Fourth Street and the steel-blue eyes of Daniel Craig stare back at you from among a more recent group of drawings. Sardi's became known as *the* pre- and post-theater dining establishment on Broadway, catering to many stage stars and producers. It's been featured in *The Country Girl*, *Please Don't Eat the Daisies*, *The King of Comedy*, and in the lyrics of the song "I Wanna Be a Producer" from *The Producers*: "I wanna be a producer/With a Hit Show on Broadway/I Wanna Be a Producer/Lunch at Sardi's every day."

While in Lower Manhattan, Keep an Eye Out for . . .

The James A. Farley Building,

a branch of the US Postal Service, opened across from the old Penn Station in 1912 on the south side of Thirty-Third Street and Eighth Avenue. It still stands, a beaux-arts beauty, and it's where the postal workers who come up with the plan to save Kris Kringle in *Miracle on 34th Street* (1947) worked. It's also featured in *The Naked City* (1949).

THE TIMES SQUARE TIME FORGOT

You'd hardly know it now, because Times Square today exudes such a family-friendly aura, but not too many decades ago, this was a place to avoid for safety reasons. Yes, it looked much the same—except for the sex shops, porno theaters, and strip clubs that occupied storefronts instead of the Disney Store and M&Ms shop. Partly that was due to the presence of nearby Hell's Kitchen, a neighborhood that since Prohibition was the most dangerous in New York, until gentrification completely remade it in the early '90s as happened to so much of the city. Watch *Midnight Cowboy* and *Taxi Driver* (1976) and you'll see a Times Square that is rundown and full of businesses of ill repute.

There's even a whiff of the seediness that's beginning to appear in Times Square in the version of the crossroads that was re-created on a soundstage for Joseph L. Mankiewicz's production of *Guys and Dolls* in 1955. Bookies are everywhere, gangsters find this their playground, and Jean Simmons's Sister Sarah Brown leads missionary campaigns against liquor and vice (she really needed to!). By the end of the '90s, Times Square seemed like a kids' theme park by comparison: clean, safe, and arguably stripped of some of its character.

The opening of *Guys and Dolls* features a largely dialogue-free musical number in which Michael Kidd's dynamic choreography introduces the hustle and bustle of Times Square—a setting featured throughout the film, including the wedding finale, pictured here.

Map It! MIDTOWN MANHATTAN

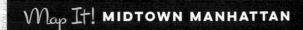

Central Park Zoo
Wollman Rink
Pierre Hotel
Plaza Hotel
ussian Tea Room
Tiffany & Co.
21 Club
Marilyn Monroe street vent for *The Seven Year Itch*
Radio City Music Hall and Rainbow Room
Waldorf-Astoria Hotel
Jimmy's Corner
Times Square
Grand Central
United Nations
New York Public Library
npire State Bldg
MIDTOWN
MURRAY HILL
KIPS BAY
EAST RIVER
QUEENSBORO BRIDGE
QUEENS-MIDTOWN TUNNEL
FRANKLIN DELANO ROOSEVELT DR
BRYANT PARK
MADISON SQUARE
FRICK COLLECTION
HUNTER COLLEGE
ROCKEFELLER UNIVERSITY

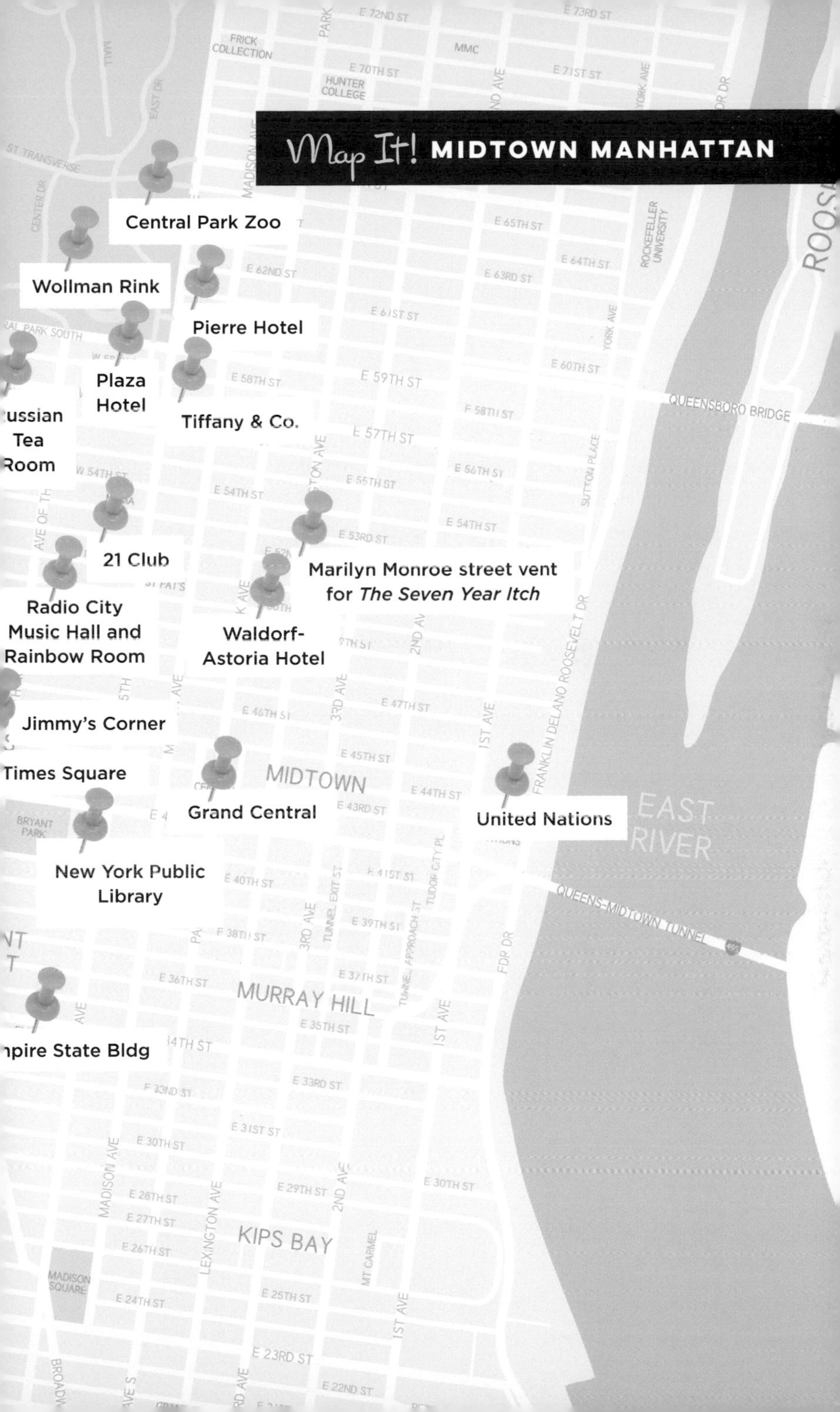

CENTRAL PARK

Cyd Charisse and Fred Astaire enchant during the "Dancing in the Dark" number, set in the middle of Central Park, in *The Band Wagon* (1953).

New
York
City

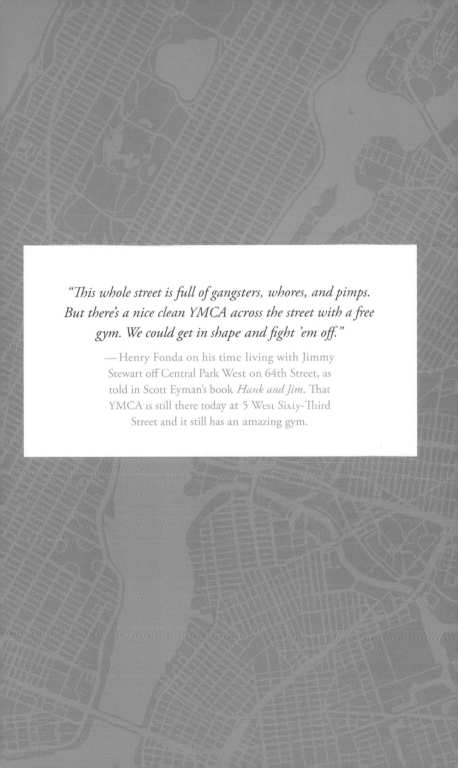

"This whole street is full of gangsters, whores, and pimps. But there's a nice clean YMCA across the street with a free gym. We could get in shape and fight 'em off."

— Henry Fonda on his time living with Jimmy Stewart off Central Park West on 64th Street, as told in Scott Eyman's book *Hank and Jim*. That YMCA is still there today at 5 West Sixty-Third Street and it still has an amazing gym.

COVERING 843 ACRES, CENTRAL PARK is an oasis, a respite from the traffic and noise of the city around it. Once you hit this sea of green at Fifty-Ninth Street, you know you've left Midtown behind. It's practically a world unto itself, with all manner of waterways, a zoo, a theater, a landmark restaurant, even a castle. Central Park required its designer, Frederick Law Olmsted, to order the use of more gunpowder to blast into its rock features and reshape the terrain than was used in the entirety of the Battle of Gettysburg.

One way to enter this quiet place is via a horse-drawn carriage, and many coachmen and their steeds await your business along Fifty-Ninth Street, also known as Central Park South. That's how Fred Astaire and Cyd Charisse arrive in Central Park in *The Band Wagon*. They leave their horse-drawn carriage behind to go for a little stroll deeper into the park and in a clearing they dance to "Dancing in the Dark," beautifully choreographed by, in this writer's opinion, the greatest New York choreographer ever, Michael Kidd, who also directed

Corie Bratter (Jane Fonda) shouts to passerby "We just got married!" as she and her new husband Paul (Robert Redford) ride in a horse-drawn carriage through Central Park to the Plaza Hotel in *Barefoot in the Park*.

the dance numbers in *Guys and Dolls*. At the end of the "Dancing in the Dark" number Fred and Cyd climb back into their horse-drawn carriage and let themselves be driven off into the night. We meet newlyweds Corie and Paul Bratter (Jane Fonda and Robert Redford) for the first time at the beginning of *Barefoot in the Park* in a horse-drawn carriage of their own that's just leaving Central Park, following their nuptials, and heading to their destination, the Plaza Hotel, where they'll spend their honeymoon. With more ominous overtones, Orson Welles's Michael meets Rita Hayworth's Elsa in Central Park at the start of *The Lady from Shanghai* (1947) after ruffians accost her in a horse-drawn carriage and he chases them off. That fateful meeting will put them both on a dark path.

Near the park's southeastern corner, within easy walking distance of the Plaza Hotel, is Wollman Rink, a beloved Manhattan oasis for ice skaters. In *Love Story* (1970), Ali MacGraw's Jennifer watches Ryan O'Neal's Oliver skate while she sits on the bleacher seating nearby

At the Central Park Zoo, Irena (Simone Simon) sketches a panther much like the kind she's been cursed to turn into whenever overcome by emotion in *Cat People* (1942).

for those who don't want to hit the ice themselves. "I like to watch you dodge and weave," she tells him. More obsessively, Jack Nicholson's Jonathan fixates on a figure skater at Wollman Rink in *Carnal Knowledge* (1971)—she's a symbol of a purer form of romance he could have but chooses not to pursue. It's also the nighttime setting of the very happy ending to *Serendipity* (2001). And nearby, at the pond, which edges up against Central Park South and is a beloved haven for the city's ducks and geese, Anne Hathaway assisted a photo shoot of models wearing eccentric carnival masks for her fashion magazine in *The Devil Wears Prada* (2006).

One of the earliest films ever shot on location in New York City, *Mounted Police Charge*, was filmed for the Edison Company by cameraman William Heise in October 1896 right in Central Park. It showed a group of NYPD officers on horseback cantering toward the camera in formation as part of an exercise. Watching the film, which is only twenty seconds long and available online, the ending of a movie from 107 years later may come to mind: it's much the way the mounted Central Park Rangers pursue a downed Santa Claus and his reindeer at the end of *Elf*.

There are a lot of fun things to do in this oasis. You could go to the Central Park Zoo on the Fifth Avenue side of the park, where director Peter Jackson shows us a number of simians at the beginning of his version of *King Kong*. The Jacqueline Kennedy Onassis Reservoir has a long jogging path as its circumference, where we see Dustin Hoffman running in *Marathon Man* (1976)—it remains as good a place as any in New York City to get a little fresh air and exercise.

At the Lake, which stretches from Seventy-Second to Seventy-Eighth Street, people rent rowboats and paddleboats to go for a little spin in the water. At the Loeb Boathouse, where there is a restaurant of the same name, ex-soldier Raymond Shaw (Laurence Harvey), whose brainwashing by Chinese intelligence operatives during the Korean War has just been prematurely activated, jumps into the Lake in *The Manchurian Candidate* (1962). At the Bethesda Fountain, Alvy (Woody Allen) and Annie (Diane Keaton) enjoyed a bit of people-

Van Johnson's Arthur, a soldier on leave in *Miracle in the Rain* (1956), meets a former tycoon who lost everything in the Crash of '29 at Central Park's Conservatory Water, where people race model sailboats—Arthur writes a human-interest story about him for the *New York Times*, with the agreement that he will be considered for a reporting job there after World War II ends.

Giselle (Amy Adams) leads a procession of singers and dancers through Central Park in *Enchanted* and enjoys the boats that people can rent on the Lake.

watching in *Annie Hall* (1977), even spotting one guy Alvy calls "the winner of the Truman Capote lookalike contest"—it was actually Capote himself in an uncredited role. The Mall is a wide thoroughfare leading up to Bethesda Terrace, which overlooks the fountain, and it's at the Mall where Dustin Hoffman teaches his son how to ride a bike in *Kramer vs. Kramer* (1979). And people race model sailboats at the Conservatory Water, an event E. B. White dramatized in his children's novel *Stuart Little* and that appears in the 1999 movie adaptation.

THE METROPOLITAN MUSEUM OF ART
1000 Fifth Avenue

It's natural to think of Central Park as an outdoor experience, but within its boundaries is the potential for days' worth of indoor fun at the greatest and grandest art museum in the country, the Metropolitan Museum of Art. Don't in any way delude yourself into thinking you can see everything there is to see at "the Met," as it's more commonly called, in a day. This is the kind of institution so massive that locals make repeated trips over years, until they've figured out the best ways to "hack" it and follow just their favorite paths through its winding galleries. That's what we see Billy Crystal's Harry and Meg Ryan's Sally do in *When Harry Met Sally . . .*, when they wander into the Temple of Dendur, an actual ancient Egyptian religious site that was taken apart and reassembled in New York exactly as it was excavated back in Egypt. This is where Harry challenges Sally to talk in a silly voice the whole day. Robert Walker and Judy Garland also have a date at the Met in *The Clock*, while Angie Dickinson pursues an intriguing stranger here in *Dressed to Kill* (1980). And Pierce Brosnan's Thomas Crown steals Claude Monet's *San Giorgio Maggiore at Dusk* here in John McTiernan's remake of *The Thomas Crown Affair* (1999).

Though not confined within the boundaries of Central Park like the Met, many visitors also end up visiting the American Museum of Natural History, bordering along Central Park West. Woody Allen's Isaac and Diane Keaton's Mary escape the rain there in *Manhattan* to tour some exhibits and visit the Hayden Planetarium, also located at the museum. There's a great scene set there in *On the Town*, which had to be filmed entirely on a soundstage, since Gene Kelly, Frank Sinatra, Ann Miller, and company end up destroying a dinosaur, *Bringing Up Baby*–style. Speaking of which, *Bringing Up Baby* (1938) is probably set here, too, though the name of the museum is never mentioned in the film. And this is the museum in question in *Night at the Museum* (2006). Denzel Washington's Malcolm X and Angela Bassett's Betty Dean Sanders (later Betty Shabazz) have their first date at the American Museum of Natural History, as depicted in Spike Lee's *Malcolm X* (1992).

Central Park, Keep an Eye Out for . . .

The Lutheran Church at 51 Central Park West

where Jack Lemmon and Sandy Dennis are kicked out, even though they just want to take a moment for spiritual reflection in *The Out-of-Towners* (1970).

Where to Eat:
Tavern on the Green

The historical value alone justifies the pricey menu of this restaurant near the southwest corner of Central Park. Tavern on the Green was extensively featured in one of Tyrone Power's last films, the poignant *Eddy Duchin Story* (1956), where it stood in for another restaurant that had been in Central Park but closed in the 1930s, the Central Park Casino (gambling did not actually take place there, and the use of "casino" in this case was a derivation of the Italian word for "little house").

Rick Moranis's specter-hunter Louis is chased by a demon at the Tavern on the Green in *Ghostbusters*. The ending of *Stella* (1990), the remake of the Barbara Stanwyck classic *Stella Dallas* (1937), occurs here with Bette Midler's Stella waiting outside and gazing in as the daughter she let go to have a better life gets married. And the wedding reception for Barbra Streisand's sister in *The Mirror Has Two Faces* (1996) takes place in the gorgeous lantern-lit garden terrace where the restaurant offers outdoor dining.

In *Crimes and Misdemeanors* (1989) the obnoxious TV producer Lester (Alan Alda), who dines at the Tavern on the Green, is believed to have been based on *M*A*S*H* showrunner Larry Gelbart.

Bandleader Eddy Duchin used to perform at the Central Park Casino, which was founded in the 1860s as a restaurant for unaccompanied ladies to the park before eventually admitting men as well. He's played by Tyrone Power in *The Eddy Duchin Story*.

HUDSON
RIVER

W 87TH ST

W 85TH ST

BROADWAY

AMSTERD

W 83RD ST

UPPER
WEST
SIDE

W 80TH S

WEST END AVE

W 79TH ST

W 78TH ST

W 75TH ST

W 76TH ST

RIVERSIDE DR

W 73RD ST

W 74TH ST

W 72ND ST

W 70TH ST

FREEDOM PL

RIVERSIDE BLVD

COLUMBUS AVE

W 69

W 68TH ST

W 67TH

W 66TH ST

W 65TH ST

W 64TH ST

AMSTERDAM AVE

BROADWAY

LINCOLN
CENTER FOR
PERFORMING
ARTS

HENRY HUDSON PARKWAY

W 63RD ST

W 61ST

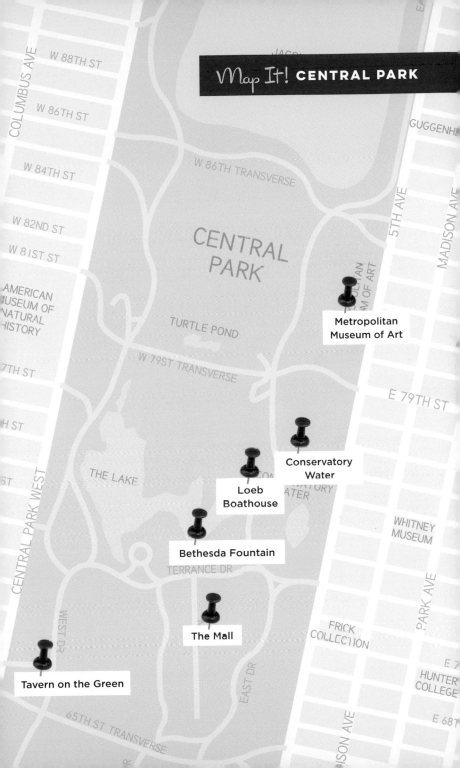

UPTOWN MANHATTAN

Russ Tamblyn's Riff and his fellow Jets prowl the Upper West Side in *West Side Story* (1961).

"I get out of the taxi and it's probably the only city which in reality looks better than on the postcards, New York."

—Miloš Forman

IF LOWER MANHATTAN IS WHERE SETTLERS in New York start out, and Midtown is where they go when they've made it, then the Upper West Side and Upper East Side are where they settle down. There's a neighborhood feel once you journey north of Fifty-Ninth Street, no matter what side of Central Park you're on.

West Side Story was filmed on location in the Upper West Side's San Juan Hill neighborhood, home to tens of thousands of Puerto Rican immigrants by the 1950s.

Ma and Pa Kettle (Marjorie Main and Percy Kilbride) get on a tour bus at Columbus Circle during their visit to New York in *Ma and Pa Kettle Go to Town* (1950).

THE UPPER WEST SIDE

There's a real neighborhood feel here: the Upper West Side is relaxed, and if there is any hint of pretention, it's more a vibe of intellectualism (or pseudo-intellectualism) rather than the moneyed status-consciousness of the Upper East Side. This is where you want to spend a rainy day in a cozy bookshop or café, have a quiet dinner at a little trattoria, or walk down to Lincoln Center to catch an opera. It's Neil Simon territory, and walking down Columbus Avenue today the atmosphere feels homey and lived in, much like it does when you're watching *The Goodbye Girl* (1977). It's an escape: a laid-back atmosphere that's just the respite you need if you've been working all day in Midtown. It's here you feel like you can breathe, and just . . . live.

In *Ghostbusters*, the specter-fighters go into battle at Columbus Circle.

Margot Kidder's Lois Lane interviews Superman from the terrace of her apartment in *Superman: The Movie*. It's only their second meeting, after they met when he rescued her when falling off the roof of a building.

The gateway to the Upper West Side is Columbus Circle. It's a large traffic roundabout that was first conceived by Central Park's designer and landscape architect Frederick Law Olmsted in 1857. It still anchors the southwest corner of Central Park the way Grand Army Plaza and the Plaza Hotel mark the southeast. It's frenetic here, as it taps into the traffic of Midtown.

In short, Columbus Circle is a place for meetings and partings, much like what you see at the end of *Crocodile Dundee*, which takes place here: Linda Kozlowski's Sue chases after Mick (Paul Hogan) after he enters the northern Columbus Circle subway station at Sixtieth Street and Broadway. He thinks she doesn't love him and he's going to leave New York City to go on "walkabout" across America. Stuck in the middle of a massive group of commuters —maybe a tad more sardine-packed than you'll usually find on a subway platform—a group of New Yorkers relay Sue's message to Mick: she loves him. He then crowd-surfs his way back to her.

One of the loveliest such meetings ever to be in a superhero film occurs at Columbus Circle in *Superman: The Movie*. Margot Kidder's reporter Lois Lane conducts an interview with Superman on the landing of her rooftop apartment—*The Daily Planet* must pay its journalists very well!— after he comes flying right in. Her apartment

Secret Service agents spot Travis Bickle (Robert De Niro) suspiciously keeping one hand in his jacket while at a Columbus Circle rally for presidential candidate Senator Charles Palantine in *Taxi Driver* (1976).

is at 240 Central Park South and, standing across the street from it, you can see very clearly its rooftop apartment today.

Columbus Circle's role as a gathering place figures into *Taxi Driver* as well. In front of the statue commemorating the victims of the USS *Maine* disaster, Senator Charles Palantine leads a political rally: he's launching a presidential bid. Thinking him a phony, Travis Bickle (Robert De Niro) attends the rally and sarcastically claps during Palantine's speech. Bickle plans on assassinating Palantine at one of these public speeches.

LINCOLN CENTER
10 Lincoln Center Plaza

The Metropolitan Opera has its home at Lincoln Center. But that's just the beginning at this one-of-a-kind campus for the arts, which also hosts the New York City Ballet, the American Ballet Theater, a theater that always features a Broadway-style show, a symphony hall, a chamber music society, and one of the best repertory cinemas in Manhattan, Film at Lincoln Center. You can imagine how enchanting all of this must have been for Cher's Loretta in *Moonstruck* (1987), when she attended her first opera here as the date of Nicolas Cage's Ronny. Ascending its red-carpeted stairs with its unique starburst chandeliers hanging overhead, you feel like you're being transported to a fantasy realm. The Metropolitan Opera moved to Lincoln Center in 1966, after having been located in an opera house at Thirty-Ninth Street and Broadway. And standing near the fountain outside, Leo Bloom (Gene Wilder) has his moment of epiphany that, yes, he will join shady producer Max Bialystock (Zero Mostel) to create the worst Broadway musical of all time in *The Producers* (1968). "I'll do it," he shouts, as the fountain suddenly erupts. Al Pacino's corruption-fighting cop had a more artistically fulfilling experience when he attended a ballet at Lincoln Center in *Serpico* (1973).

There had been attempts to move the Met to a different location dating back to the late 1920s—negotiations fell through to create an opera house on the site of what became Radio City Music Hall, which would have been one of the first buildings in

In *Moonstruck*, Nicolas Cage's Ronny takes Cher's Loretta to the Metropolitan Opera at Lincoln Center to see a performance of Puccini's *La Bohème*.

Rockefeller Center. Many films are set at "The Old Met," as it was called, on Thirty-Ninth Street, including part of the Nelson Eddy/Jeanette MacDonald musical *Maytime* (1937), based on the Sigmund Romberg operetta and one of MGM's most beautiful films of the 1930s—one of the last boy-wonder producer Irving Thalberg oversaw before his death.

Spotlight on West Side Story (1961)

Because the area around Lincoln Square, known as San Juan Hill, was full of tenement housing for low-income, often immigrant, families in the 1950s, it made the perfect setting for *West Side Story*, which made its debut on Broadway in 1957 and was released as a film four years later. For the film, director Robert Wise and choreographer Jerome Robbins (who was given a co-director credit because of the importance of dance in telling the story) filmed on location in and around San Juan Hill, where the story is set, to tell this tale of love tragically caught between rival gangs.

The actor-dancers who portray one of the gangs in the film, the Jets, perform on location on the West Side. You can see almost nothing from *West Side Story* in person today, as almost all the locations were torn down to make way for the construction of Lincoln Center.

Jerome Robbins directs George Chakiris and actor-dancers playing two other Sharks. When all the tenements around Lincoln Square were demolished to make way for Lincoln Center, almost seven thousand low-income residents were ousted from the neighborhood, according to the *New York Times*.

Robert Wise wanted Jerome Robbins to direct all the dance sequences in the movie himself, since Wise had never tried his hand at a musical before. They were both credited as the film's directors, despite Robbins being fired a third of the way into the production. However, both won the Academy Award for Best Director.

Robbins acts out a key moment in the Sharks' dance early in the film. After he was fired from the production, he almost suffered a nervous breakdown.

Posh Upper West Siders were still displeased, even after the urban renewal efforts that brought Lincoln Center to fruition, because drug addicts congregated in Verdi Square, nicknamed "Needle Park," as depicted in *The Panic in Needle Park* (1971). Verdi Square was previously seen in *The Naked City* (1948).

DESIGN FOR LIVING

Most of the Upper West Side is strictly residential. That means a lot of the stores and restaurants you'll find here are not geared to tourists but to locals. Zabar's (2245 Broadway) is a combination grocery store and coffee shop/bakery where the lines are long but the waits are always worth it. Melissa McCarthy's Lee Israel and Richard E. Grant's Jack Hock in *Can You Ever Forgive Me?* (2018) buy loaves of French bread here that are still warm and soft as they take bites out of them while walking down the street. Tom Hanks and Meg Ryan shop there in *You've Got Mail* (1998).

Incidentally, the storefront that served as Meg Ryan's bookstore, the Shop Around the Corner, in *You've Got Mail* is located at 109

West Sixty-Ninth Street. Shortly thereafter, it became one of the locations of La Mode Organic Dry Cleaners, again reflecting how the businesses you'll find here cater to residents. Likewise, what was once the Emerald Inn bar featured in *The Apartment* (1960) is now a store, though there's a newer iteration of the Emerald Inn on Seventy-Second Street near West End Avenue.

In *You've Got Mail* (1999), Meg Ryan's Kathleen Kelly accidentally gets into the "cash only" line at Zabar's. The customers behind her are not pleased, but then, with a wink and a smile, her frenemy-turned-romantic-interest Joe Fox (Tom Hanks) charms the cashier into accepting her credit card.

You've Got Mail was Nora Ephron's update of Ernst Lubitsch's *The Shop Around the Corner* (1940), the title of which lends its name to the bookstore owned by Meg Ryan's Kathleen Kelly.

Where to Eat:
Café Lalo

This adorable dessert place on Eighty-Third Street between Broadway and Amsterdam Avenue has a bit of a laid-back European character. With most places in New York City you're seated quickly, but then have to make up your mind and order quickly, too. Here you can relax, especially since it's open late. Brunch is served until 4:00 p.m. each day and you can get small plates, sandwiches, and salads at practically any time, but you really come here for your sweet tooth: the affogato, the zabaglione, the Napoleon, twenty varieties of cheesecakes. Expect some of the more elaborate desserts to come with a cordial poured over it or baked into it—there's even a Grand Marnier cake. This is also just a good place to enjoy slowly sipping an after-dinner cognac or nibbling on a cheese plate. And it's an ideal date spot: that's what Meg Ryan's Kathleen had in mind in *You've Got Mail*. She finally arranged with her online pen pal to meet in person, with a red rose in her book, and got all settled in at a table. Her date, Tom Hanks's Joe is too scared to go in and meet her. He asks his friend Kevin (Dave Chappelle) to peek in through the window and describe what she looks like to him. Kevin is shocked by what he sees: "You know what? She looks . . . I mean she almost has the same coloring as . . . that Kathleen Kelly . . . if you don't like Kathleen Kelly I can tell you right now you ain't gonna like this girl . . . Because it is Kathleen Kelly." Nora and Delia Ephron lightly reworked that dialogue from Samson Raphaelson's original script for Lubitsch's first version of this story, *The Shop Around the Corner*. Joe decides to walk away (for a moment, anyway), since he and Kathleen have engaged in a feud. While Kathleen sits at her table waiting for him, it's hilarious to see her looking at the men who walk in, with her thinking that each one could be "the one."

THE DAKOTA
1 West Seventy-Second Street

Even before you learn about all its history, you're struck by it. The Dakota is like a horror movie director's take on an English High Renaissance palace. With its gables and dormers and dark stone walls, it would be what F. W. Murnau would've built if he had abandoned filmmaking for architecture. And then once you've heard its history— or see *Rosemary's Baby*—you truly never forget it.

The architect who designed the Plaza Hotel, Henry Janeway Hardenbergh, built the Dakota more than twenty years before the iconic hotel. It opened in 1884 overlooking Central Park at West Seventy-Second Street, and if you look at photos of it from that time it's extraordinary: it's surrounded by nothing. It looks like a mini-skyscraper in the middle of nowhere. Ten floors high, the luxury building offered sixty-five apartments for sale, which were snapped up right away, despite it being in such a remote and undeveloped part of the city. And that odd location is how it got its name. Christopher Gray quoted a 1933 newspaper clipping of the Dakota's longtime original manager in his book *New York Streetscapes*: "Probably it was called 'Dakota' because it was so far west and so far north." For visitors traveling from downtown, the building might as well have been in the Dakota territory.

The building is immortalized in *Rosemary's Baby* (1968) as the place where young married couple Rosemary and Guy Woodhouse move in while Guy pursues his acting career in New York. In the film it's called the Bramford, but production designer Richard Sylbert wanted to film at the Dakota—only the exteriors of the Dakota serve to represent the Bramford, though, as its owners refused interior filming. But that exterior, with its dark hues and jagged edges and quasi-Gothic or Renaissance feel was perfect. This was a place where elderly Satan worshippers might indeed live and conspire to get Rosemary pregnant with the Lord of Darkness's spawn—her own husband, Guy, is in on the plot against her so he can advance his acting career.

The Dakota is also where John Lennon lived with his wife, Yoko Ono, throughout much of the 1970s, and where, in front of its main

Rosemary and Guy Woodhouse (Mia Farrow and John Cassavetes) walk through the main entrance at The Dakota—the courtyard within can only be accessed by residents.

entrance, he was shot and killed on December 8, 1980. A commemorative sing-along in honor of Lennon takes place in the shadow of the Dakota in Central Park's Strawberry Fields (named after his song with the Beatles) every December 8.

So many others with Hollywood connections lived at the Dakota: Judy Garland, Rosemary Clooney and José Ferrer, Lillian Gish, Boris Karloff, Robert Ryan, Jack Palance, Rosie O'Donnell, Jason Robards, and Leonard Bernstein. A year after her death in 2014, the *New York Times* reported Lauren Bacall's nine-bedroom apartment sold for $21 million.

It's also possible The Dakota is where Maureen O'Hara's Doris Walker lives with her daughter Susan (Natalie Wood) in *Miracle on 34th Street*. Their neighbor, attorney Fred Gailey, has a view of Central Park West, right on the Macy's Thanksgiving Day Parade route, where he and Susan enjoy watching all the balloons float by. But more than likely they live at 55 Central Park West, at 66th Street, where James Caan's Walter Hobbs, the father of Buddy the Elf (Will Ferrell) lives in *Elf*. The building at 55 Central Park West is also "Spook Central" in *Ghostbusters*, being the apartment building of Sigourney Weaver's cellist. Built in 1929, and the first Art Deco building on Central Park West, Ginger Rogers lived here in the early 1930s when she performed on Broadway.

— 2109 Broadway —

While on the Upper West Side, Keep an Eye Out for . . .

The Ansonia, a beaux-arts apartment building, and initially a residential hotel, built in 1899. It's where Walter Matthau's Willy lives in *The Sunshine Boys* (1975). In real life, Chicago White Sox first baseman Chick Gandil lived at the Ansonia and in his apartment he held meetings with his fellow players to persuade them to join in on "throwing" the 1919 World Series.

THE UPPER EAST SIDE

Where the Upper West Side is laid-back and a bit reserved, the Upper East Side is all about display: the grand habitat of the wealthy and powerful, full of eye-popping Gilded Age mansions and some of New York City's swankiest hotels. You go to the Upper West Side to feel cozy, you go to the Upper East Side to feel chic. If you want to get a sense of how the wealthiest people in the world lived during the boom period of the late nineteenth century, known as the Gilded Age, go visit the Frick Collection right on Fifth Avenue at 1 East Seventieth Street, once the mansion of industrialist Henry Clay Frick. It's a small art museum with a pretty impressive batting average when it comes to masterpieces. Or visit the Cooper Hewitt, Smithsonian Design Museum that's been located in the Carnegie Mansion at 2 East Ninety-First Street since 1976. Steel magnate Andrew Carnegie had it built from 1899 to 1902, and it was where he retired in his later years to spend his time on his philanthropic endeavors. In fact, the surrounding neighborhood was named Carnegie Hill after him.

Visiting the Frick or Carnegie mansions gives you a sense of what it would be like to live in the kind of imposing, palace-like home where Katharine Hepburn's Linda Seton grew up in *Holiday* (1938). You'll have a taste of the Fifth Avenue splendor hobo Aloysius T. McKeever (Victor Moore) in *It Happened on Fifth Avenue* (1947) would experience each winter when he breaks into the mansion a millionaire abandons each year when he heads south. Lonely millionaire Timothy Borden (Walter Connolly) in *Fifth Avenue Girl* (1939) lives in luxury, but despite all his riches he feels lonely—his wife is cheating on him and his children are neglectful. When he meets an unemployed young woman (Ginger Rogers) who barely has enough to eat, he can't help but invite her out to dinner, and then she becomes a houseguest at his Fifth Avenue mansion, where she shakes up his life for good.

If you've got money to spare and are looking to have a taste of the luxury that was second nature to Walter Connolly in *Fifth Avenue Girl*, consider a stay at the Pierre Hotel on Sixty-First Street and Fifth Avenue. In *Joe Versus the Volcano* (1990), Tom Hanks's Joe, who thinks he only has a short time to live, asks his driver Marshall (Ossie Davis) if he should stay at the Plaza because he wants to stay in a fancy hotel. "The Plaza's nice . . . I'd go to the Pierre," Marshall replies. In *Holiday Inn* (1942), it's likely that Fred Astaire's Ted Hanover and Virginia Dale's Lila Dixon perform here—their friend Jim (Bing Crosby) comes to watch them at the Club Pierre, which likely just meant the Pierre Hotel. It was under the management of oil tycoon J. Paul Getty at the time in 1942 and entering a new renaissance.

George Cukor's *Holiday* stars Cary Grant as a working-class striver who finds out a bit too late that his fiancée is fantastically wealthy and grew up in an Upper East Side mansion. Joining this family means giving up his more carefree dreams and joining the family business, which he ultimately realizes isn't for him—though he may just be right for his fiancée's sister, Katharine Hepburn.

The Carlyle Hotel on Seventy-Sixth Street and Madison Avenue may exceed even the Pierre in terms of sheer star power: Michael Jackson and Princess Diana were regulars, and Mick Jagger owns an apartment here—though it has 190 rental rooms and suites, it also has sixty apartments that can be bought by megawealthy patrons who want all the amenities of a hotel. The Café Carlyle, a popular venue for old jazz standards and Great American Songbook staples, is featured prominently in *Hannah and Her Sisters* (1986), as is its longtime resident singer, Bobby Short, who died in 2005 after a career as one of the finest interpreters of the Great American Songbook tradition ever, singing a Cole Porter classic.

MOON RIVER AND ME . . .

The Upper East Side is all about wealth and glamour—but people who aren't millionaires or billionaires have been known to live here, too. Katharine Hepburn's Bunny Watson resides in an apartment on Lexington Avenue—pronounced "Mexican Avenue" when drunk following an office Christmas party—in this vicinity in *Desk Set*. She lets Spencer Tracy's Richard Sumner dry off here when they're caught in the rain, even letting him wear the bathrobe she was going to give to her boyfriend (Gig Young). Then she prepares fried chicken and a dessert of floating islands. What could be better?

Nearby, at 169 East Seventy-First Street, you'll find the walk-up town-house apartment where Audrey Hepburn's Holly Golightly lived in *Breakfast at Tiffany's* (1961). It's chic enough to look like it could be in Paris, with its dainty white facade, light brown steps, and black door with just a hint of green. Unfortunately, the town house was left in disrepair for some years. But recently it was fixed up and sold for nearly $6 million.

This is also right near where Melissa McCarthy's Lee Israel lives in *Can You Ever Forgive Me?* in far less fashionable lodgings. Her favorite diner, Neil's Coffee Shop, is still located on the corner of Seventieth and Lexington. In New York City, a "coffee shop" is usually code for a full-service diner—and at this one, Lee and her coconspirator Jack Hock (Richard E. Grant) would discuss her

Katharine Hepburn's Bunny Watson lets Spencer Tracy's Richard Summer escape the rain at her Lexington Avenue apartment in *Desk Set*—unfortunately, her insensitive boyfriend, Gig Young's Mike Cutler, crashes the party.

criminal scheme to sell forged letters attributed to literary celebrities. And a little farther uptown at Eighty-Third Street and York Avenue, you'll find Logos Bookstore, the workplace of Dolly Wells's Anna, with whom Lee shares a few flirty moments before Lee's caught for her forgery scheme.

Third Avenue in the Upper East Side was decidedly less posh in the first half of the twentieth century than other parts of the neighborhood because an elevated subway train ran here until 1955. People

José Luis de Vilallonga's José da Silva Periera drops off Audrey Hepburn's Holly Golightly at her town house apartment in Breakfast at *Tiffany's.*

who couldn't afford cars and needed the easy access of public transit lived here. The Third Avenue El figures prominently in *The Lost Weekend*, especially when Ray Milland's Don Birnam tries visiting a string of pawnshops that were located here. According to Gene Phillips's book *Some Like It Wilder*, director Billy Wilder tried to achieve maximum authenticity in the shots of Don walking down the street by hiding his camera on the back of trucks or behind objects so that no one around Milland would know a movie was being filmed. There's no elevated track there today, but if you stand at Third Avenue and Seventy-Fifth Street, you'll be right where Don Birnam took a moment to collect himself while still desperately trying to find a place to hock his typewriter for drinking money.

THE SOLOMON R. GUGGENHEIM MUSEUM
1071 Fifth Avenue

It looks like an alien spaceship that's just landed on Eighty-Eighth Street and Fifth Avenue, and it was the final architectural wonder conceived by Frank Lloyd Wright—opening six months after his death in 1959. For a city that embraces more classic forms—beaux art, art deco, and neoclassical, especially—the Guggenheim is a staggering modernist punctuation mark, and as much architectural proof as anything that an incredibly striking form can follow function. Its main gallery looks like an inverted cone because it contains one long spiral ramp winding over and over itself until you have seven floors stacked upon one another like coils in a spring. It's the perfect way to display an exhibition—always rotating—of modern and contemporary work in a continuous, uninterrupted space. Diane Keaton's Mary in *Manhattan* praises a steel cube at the Guggenheim as "textural," "perfectly integrated," and possessing a "marvelous kind of negative capability." But maybe that's appropriate since the Guggenheim collection was originally called the Museum of Non-Objective Art. *Cactus Flower* (1969) and *Three Days of the Condor* (1975) also shot scenes at the Guggenheim. And it possesses another classic Hollywood connection: architect Frank Lloyd Wright's granddaughter was actress Anne Baxter, Eve herself, in *All About Eve* (1950).

While on the Upper East Side, Keep an Eye Out for . . .

JG Melon at 1291 Third Avenue, the cash-only pub known for its delicious burgers. Dustin Hoffman and Meryl Streep share a meal here in *Kramer vs. Kramer* (1979). Follow up your meal with something sweet at legendary dessert joint Serendipity 3 at 225 East Sixtieth Street, featured in *Serendipity* (2001).

HARLEM

Journey farther north still, past the northern edge of Central Park at 110th Street and you'll find one of the most culturally rich neighborhoods in all of New York City: Harlem. Named by the earliest Dutch settlers after the town of Haarlem outside Amsterdam in the Netherlands, this area of New York grew to prominence during the Great Migration of the early 1900s, when millions of African Americans moved from the American South, where they increasingly faced violence and ever more discriminatory Jim Crow laws, to cities in the North. By the end of World War I in 1918, some of the most creative black artists, writers, and musicians were living in Harlem. But at that time, no African Americans were permitted to enter what would become Harlem's most iconic institution, the Apollo Theater, which had opened in 1914 and wouldn't allow nonwhites to attend performances there until twenty years later. It was an absolute triumph then when Barry Jenkins's *If Beale Street Could Talk*, shot entirely on location in Harlem and evoking its colors and textures like almost no other film before it, had its North American debut at the Apollo Theater as part of the 2018 New York Film Festival. The tragedy of the Harlem Renaissance throughout the '20s was that when musicians like Duke Ellington, Cab Calloway, and Louis Armstrong (who all experienced Hollywood success) were performing in venues throughout Harlem, they were only performing for white audiences who had traveled uptown to hear them—the black residents who made up Harlem were shut out.

Malcolm X (Denzel Washington) speaks in front of the Apollo Theater on 125th Street in Spike Lee's *Malcolm X*.

Spike Lee's *Malcolm X* includes an exuberant dance sequence
showcasing Lindy Hoppers, the likes of which would have
performed at the Savoy Ballroom.

One especially famous nightclub in which this tragic
discrimination played out was the Cotton Club. Located at 142nd
Street and Lenox Avenue, it opened in 1923 and featured Fletcher
Henderson, Ethel Waters, Bessie Smith, Bill Robinson (maybe best
known today for his dance numbers in several Shirley Temple movies),
and the Nicholas Brothers. Fayard and Harold Nicholas brought
an acrobatic flair to their dancing that inspires exclamations from
anyone who watches them of "How did they do that?" The Cotton
Club launched their Hollywood career and they appeared in films like
The Big Broadcast of 1936 (1935), *Sun Valley Serenade* (1941), *Down
Argentine Way* (1940), *Stormy Weather* (1943), and *The Pirate* (1948).
The Associated Press reports Gregory Hines once said that if a biopic
were made of the Nicholas Brothers' lives, the dancing scenes would

require CGI body doubles, because no dancer alive could replicate the virtuosity of their flips, splits, and other death-defying dancing feats. But all people of color were barred from patronizing the Cotton Club, and that racism wasn't left behind when they went to Hollywood. The Nicholas Brothers' dance numbers onscreen were usually standalone scenes disconnected from the plot so they could be easily edited out when the films would play in southern movie theaters.

The Cotton Club was also the site of gangland rivalries in the '20s and '30s, something dramatized in Francis Ford Coppola's 1984 film *The Cotton Club*. Its owner was Owney Madden, played by Bob Hoskins, and the film pins legendary mobster Dutch Schultz's death on Madden. By the early 1930s, Madden lost control of the Cotton Club, and it moved for a few years to a location in Midtown—but not before Lena Horne and Dorothy Dandridge, among future Hollywood stars, had performed there. Today, a new version of the Cotton Club is open for business—excluding no one—at 125th Street and Riverside Drive.

Gangster Owney Madden owned the Cotton Club and maintained a strict "whites only" policy for its clientele, even though all of its performers were black.

Just one block south of the Cotton Club was a venue that was integrated—and that arguably had the most significant impact on the music of the 1930s as any live-music hot spot in America: the Savoy Ballroom. The Savoy wasn't where big band music was created—Duke Ellington, Paul Whiteman, and Fletcher Henderson had done that elsewhere—but it was here in this massive dance space between 140th and 141st on Lenox Avenue that big band became swing, that it became the dance music craze that would spread from coast to coast. In the mid-1930s the Savoy's band leader was drummer Chick Webb, who gave an energy and a pulse to big band like no one before him. With earworms like "Stompin' at the Savoy" he could fire up the four thousand dancers who could fit in the ballroom at one time, and the dynamic dance of lifts and twirls, the Lindy Hop, was born. When Ella Fitzgerald, who had won the amateur night talent contest at the Apollo Theater in 1934, right after it integrated, joined Chick Webb's band as lead singer, the band became simply the most exciting in the country.

There were Lindy Hoppers all over Harlem, but the best of the best troupe, Whitey's Lindy Hoppers, named after Herbert "Whitey" White, were always at the Savoy. Whitey's Lindy Hoppers would even make appearances in the Marx Brothers' *A Day at the Races* (1937), *Hellzapoppin'* (1941), and *Killer Diller* (1948). No movie was ever actually filmed at the Savoy Ballroom—even though Hollywood stars like Clark Gable and Lana Turner were regulars—but you can get a very clear sense of what the vibe would have been like by watching the massive Lindy Hop dance sequence Spike Lee staged in *Malcolm X.* That dynamic sequence is supposed to be at the Roseland Ballroom in Boston, though it was actually shot at the Diplomat Ballroom in Manhattan at Forty-Third Street. But the then-seventysomething Frankie Manning, who in the 1930s was a member of Whitey's Lindy Hoppers and appeared in both *Hellzapoppin'* and *Killer Diller*, worked with Spike Lee to get the details of this sequence right and teach Denzel Washington some moves. From the entirety of its existence from 1926 to 1958, the Savoy Ballroom had a nondiscrimination policy and was integrated. Unfortunately, it was torn down some time after it closed. The Diplomat Ballroom featured in *Malcolm X* is also gone. Oddly

Roscoe Lee Brown's Philippe Dubois, a journalist moonlighting as a spy, enters the Hotel Theresa to interview an envoy for Fidel Castro's government staying there in Alfred Hitchcock's *Topaz*.

enough, Spike Lee redressed the exact same space at the Diplomat to re-create the Audubon Ballroom at 165th and Broadway, where Malcolm X was assassinated in 1965.

From 1940, the year that it finally allowed African Americans to check in, the Hotel Theresa was the place to stay in Harlem. Built in 1913 and only thirteen stories, it was a place where you could experience a bit of luxury on the cheap. Fidel Castro reserved eighty rooms at a bulk rate of $800 a day when he was visiting the UN in 1962, an event that inspired one of the most striking and memorable sequences from Alfred Hitchcock's late period. In *Topaz* (1969), Philippe Dubois (Roscoe Lee Brown), a spy working as a journalist for cover, is sent by the French foreign intelligence agency to enter the Hotel Theresa and interview a member of the delegation there. Really, he's trying to acquire some information that will prove Cuba will be receiving missile shipments from the Soviet Union. Hitchcock films this extraordinary scene using a long telephoto lens, to reflect the perspective of the French intelligence officer (Frederick Stafford) across the street watching Dubois enter the hotel, get screened by the

Cuban security, and journey up to the floor where he needs to go. It's the same filming technique he used in *Rear Window*, with a subjective camera showing exactly what the French intelligence officer across the street is seeing. Stafford's spy is in Jimmy Stewart's L. B. Jefferies role with Roscoe Lee Brown's Dubois in the same possibly dangerous position that Grace Kelly's Lisa Fremont finds herself when she sneaks into the murderer's apartment. And as in *Rear Window*, Hitchcock doesn't have any score accompany this scene but just the ambient sounds of the city. In order to film it this way, the Hotel Theresa, just like the apartment block in *Rear Window*, was completely re-created, exterior and interior, on the Universal lot in Los Angeles. In the book *Henry Bumstead and the World of Hollywood Art Direction*, Bumstead, the production designer of *Topaz*, told author Andrew Horton, "Hitch said it looked so good that everyone would think we actually filmed those scenes in New York."

From 1940, the year that it finally allowed African Americans to check in, the Hotel Theresa was located at 2070-2018 Adam Clayton Powell Jr. Boulevard. After, when African American celebrities came to New York, they often stayed there. Eddie "Rochester" Anderson was a regular, as were Lena Horne and Dorothy Dandridge. Decades later in the 2009 film *Precious*, Gabourey Sidibe's title character attends a special class on the top floor of the hotel.

COLUMBIA UNIVERSITY

The iconic campus that stretches from 114th Street to 120th between Broadway and Amsterdam Avenue and is flanked by two grand federal-style libraries, didn't even exist until 1896. Columbia was previously located on the tract of land that would become Rockefeller Center. John D. Rockefeller Jr. actually had to lease the site for Rockefeller Center for $3 million a year, and Columbia maintained its ownership of the land beneath the Center until it finally sold it to the Rockefeller Group in 1985—until that time, whenever improvements were needed to existing Rockefeller Center buildings, such as the installation of air-conditioning, Columbia University was responsible for initiating the improvements.

Tobey Maguire's Peter Parker delivers pizzas and snaps photos for the *Daily Bugle* to pay for the astronomical tuition of Columbia University in *Spider-Man 2*.

Uptown, in the neighborhood of Morningside Heights, to the south and east of Harlem, Columbia's present campus ballooned into an academic refuge in the middle of the city. It was up here where Richard Rodgers and Lorenz Hart studied and where they first met as depicted in Norman Taurog's 1948 biopic *Words and Music*. Mickey Rooney's Hart kept a spacious apartment right near the campus, where he first conjured some of the finest lyrics in the Great American Songbook, including for the song "Manhattan," as in "We'll take Manhattan / The Bronx and Staten Island too . . ." Almost fifty years later, another of the most talented musicians America has ever seen, Barbra Streisand, would play a Columbia professor in *The Mirror Has Two Faces*. In one yuletide sequence, Streisand's character and her burgeoning love interest, played by Jeff Bridges, attend a holiday concert at Columbia's chapel. Bridges's character, who's a math professor, pulls out an electronic device that turns the music—David Foster's version of "Carol of the Bells"—into a visual pattern. And Tobey Maguire's Peter Parker, a science whiz in addition to being a web-slinger, is shown to be a student at Columbia in *Spider-Man 2* (2004). But unlike Mickey Rooney's Lorenz Hart, and very much like so many actual students at Columbia, he can only afford a cramped, depressing one-room apartment while pursuing his undergraduate career. That's the thing about living in New York: you can be attending one of the finest universities in the country (which Columbia certainly is) or embarking on a career that could send you into the stratosphere, but you have to pay your dues along the way: tiny apartments can be part of that dues-paying.

While in Uptown Manhattan, Keep an Eye Out for . . .

Grant's Tomb in Riverside Park, the final resting place of Ulysses S. Grant. In *The Thin Man* (1934), Nick Charles (William Powell) tells a taxi driver to send his wife, Nora (Myrna Loy), to Grant's Tomb so as to keep her out of his way. It's at Riverside Drive and 122nd Street, so if you're walking west along Harlem's "main street," 125th Street, walk three blocks south once you catch a glimpse of the park. Head due south if you end up walking as far west as the new Cotton Club. Keep going farther south beyond Grant's Tomb and you'll be in the part of the park where Charles Bronson's Paul Kersey shoots and kills a mugger, beginning his vigilante killing spree in *Death Wish* (1974).

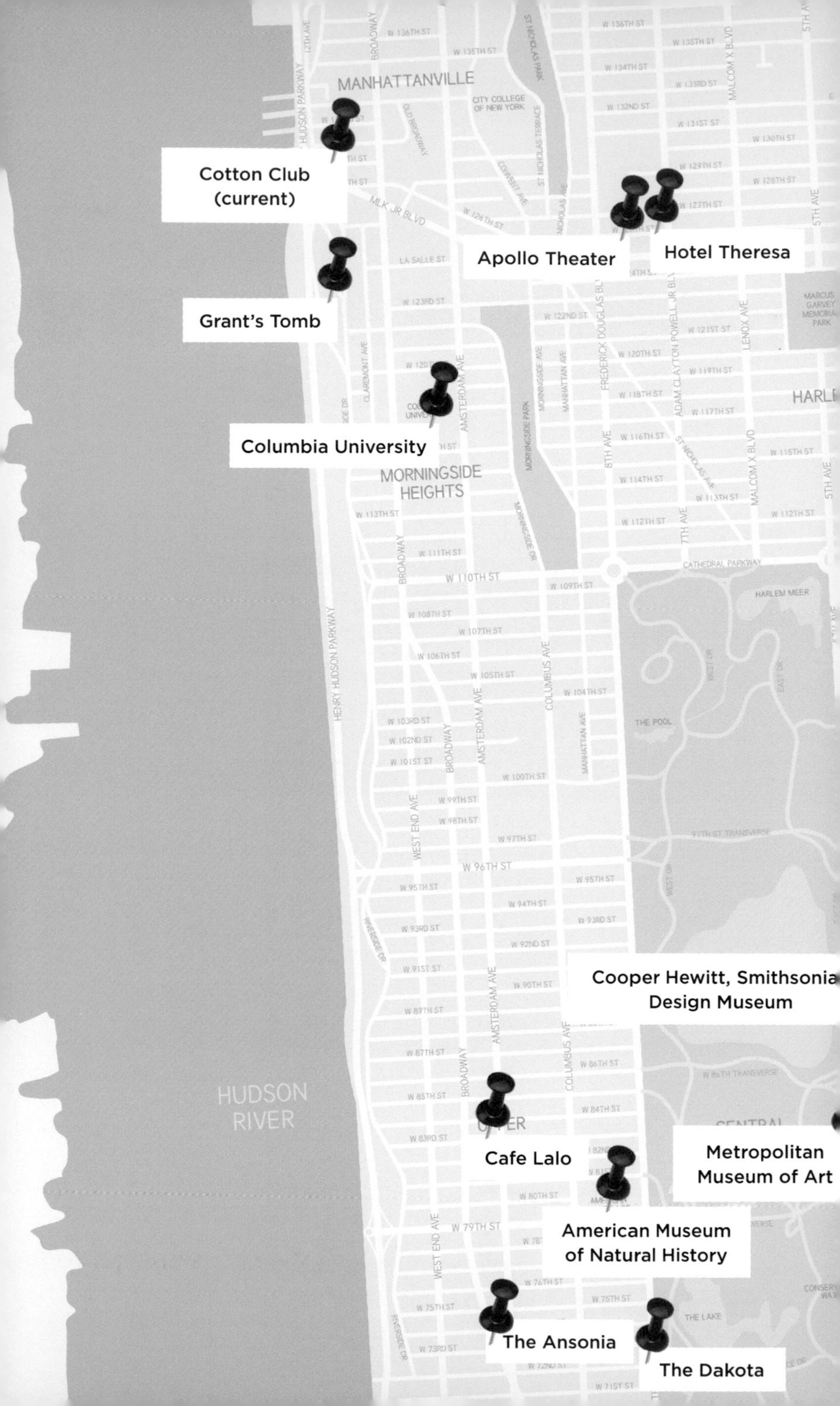

Cotton Club (current)
Grant's Tomb
Columbia University
Apollo Theater
Hotel Theresa
MANHATTANVILLE
MORNINGSIDE HEIGHTS
HUDSON RIVER
Cooper Hewitt, Smithsonia
Design Museum
Metropolitan Museum of Art
Cafe Lalo
American Museum of Natural History
The Ansonia
The Dakota

TRIBOROUGH BRIDGE

E 127TH ST

LEXINGTON AVE

3RD AVE

WILLIS AVE BRIDGE

E 125RD ST

124TH ST

E 123RD ST

B22ND ST

FDR DR

E 121ST ST

1ST AVE

PALADINO AVE

E 120TH ST

E 119TH ST

PLEASANT ST

3RD AVE

E 118TH ST

E 117TH ST

E 116TH ST

E 116TH ST

E 116TH ST

2ND AVE

E 115TH ST

E 114TH ST

WARDS ISLAND

EAST HARLEM

JEFFERSON PARK

E 112TH ST

E 111TH ST

110TH ST

E 109TH ST

E 107TH ST

E 106TH ST

FDR DR

WARDS ISLAND PARK

E 105TH ST

1ST AVE

LEXINGTON AVE

E 104TH ST

E 103RD ST

TRIBOROUGH BRIDGE

E 102ND ST

E 101ST ST

E 100TH ST

E 99TH ST

8 ST

METROPOLITAN HOSPITAL CENTER

E 96TH ST

E 97TH ST

E 96TH ST

E 95TH ST

FDR DR

E 94TH ST

E 93RD ST

MILL ROCK PARK

E 92ND ST

2ND AVE

E 91ST ST

E 90TH ST

91ST ST

YORKVILLE

E 89TH ST

97TH ST

3RD AVE

E 88TH ST

87TH ST

E 87TH ST

LEXINGTON AVE

E 86TH ST

EAST END AVE

85TH ST

E 85TH ST

E 84TH ST

83RD ST

E 82ND ST

YORK AVE

E 81ST ST

E 81ST ST

UPPER EAST SIDE

E 80TH ST

E 79TH ST

JOHN JAY PARK

E 78TH ST

1ST AVE

E 77TH ST

E 76TH ST

Carlyle Hotel

E 74TH ST

RSEUM

E 73RD ST

MMC

E 71ST ST

PARK AVE

YORK AVE

FDR DR

ROOSEVELT ISLAND

E 70TH ST

E 69TH ST

2ND AVE

HUNTER

QUEENS

Michael Corleone (Al Pacino) shares a meal at the defunct Louis Italian-American Restaurant in the Bronx with Captain McCluskey (Sterling Hayden) and Sollozzo (Al Lettieri) in *The Godfather*.

"That's my favorite place in the world, so far, that I've seen. I haven't traveled much, but I don't think I'll find anything to replace Brooklyn."

—Marilyn Monroe

NEW YORK CITY IS MADE UP OF FIVE boroughs, all of which were divided into separate cities or towns before they were consolidated into the one administrative unit that is the City of New York in 1898. Of the five boroughs, Manhattan, the great showroom of New York, is only the third most populous: Brooklyn has the most people followed by Queens, with the Bronx and Staten Island having fewer than Manhattan.

THE BRONX

If you want cheap, no-frills housing like the kind Peter Parker had in *Spider-Man 2*, you'd do well to look toward the Bronx, which has been flourishing in recent years. The image of the Bronx that movies like *Fort Apache, The Bronx* (1981) cultivated was one of relentless crime and poverty. The stories you hear about, say, the 1976 Yankee Stadium boxing match between Muhammad Ali and Ken Norton, such as how the major celebrities who attended were being robbed by pickpockets and hold-up men on the outside while fires raged in the neighborhoods around them, are now in the far distant past. Attend a game or a concert at Yankee Stadium today—alas, not the original stadium, "The House That Ruth Built," where taxi driver Harold Lloyd takes Babe Ruth (playing himself) in *Speedy* (1928), where *The Pride of the Yankees* (1942) takes place and Doris Day trades dugout quips with Yogi Berra in *That Touch of Mink* (1962)—and you'll feel perfectly safe. Poverty is still a problem, though. The Bronx has traditionally been the second stop for immigrants: the Italians and Jews who first settled in the Lower East Side in the early 1900s then moved here. You can still see many buildings along the Grand Concourse that have Hebrew characters and Stars of David cut into the stone reflecting that time.

Where to Eat:
Mario's Restaurant

With that Jewish and Italian influence in the Bronx you can see why, while Marlon Brando's Vito Corleone clings to life after being shot in *The Godfather*, his son Michael (Al Pacino) would agree to meet rival gangster Sollozzo (Al Lettieri) and the corrupt police captain McCluskey (Sterling Hayden) at a restaurant here. Of course Michael plans on killing them both. And the way to do that is by having one of his crew tape a gun behind the toilet earlier on, which Michael will then retrieve and use to shoot them while they're sitting at the table eating their veal parmesan. It's a haunting, unforgettable scene and the moment when Michael goes from being an outsider to the gangster killer who'll one day be a kingpin. Director Francis Ford Coppola filmed it at Louis Italian-American Restaurant in the Bronx. Its dark interior was perfect, but it wasn't Coppola's first choice. He wanted to film at Mario's Restaurant on Arthur Avenue, which is where the scene is set in Mario Puzo's original novel. But the owner Mario Migliucci didn't want his restaurant associated with a murder, so he refused. Mario's Restaurant is still in business, however, while Louis Italian-American Restaurant shuttered permanently not long after Coppola wrapped the production. Now is an especially good time to visit Mario's, if you want to eat where Puzo originally set the scene it celebrated its one hundreth anniversary in 2019.

Louis Italian-American Restaurant in the Bronx, defunct shortly after *The Godfather* finished filming, was the place where Michael Corleone (Al Pacino) commits his first murders.

BRONX BEGINNINGS

The neighborhood around Mario's in the Bronx is called Belmont, and *A Bronx Tale* (1993), Robert De Niro's directorial debut based on the childhood memories of actor Chazz Palminteri (who first turned this story into a play in 1989), was filmed largely in this area. As was Delbert Mann's *Marty* (1955), about a lovelorn thirty-five-year-old butcher trying to find happiness despite seemingly everyone in Belmont telling him he should be ashamed he isn't married. The opening shots of the film show the Arthur Avenue Retail Market, which still exists, is open seven days a week, and employs four butchers. Marty's shop is either nestled within the market or located right nearby. All Marty would have to do is walk two blocks north and two blocks east to his home at 2454 Belmont Avenue, the exterior of which was filmed for the movie. And if you're in a melancholy mood, head up to

Chazz Palminteri's play *A Bronx Tale* became a movie, the first Robert De Niro directed, and then a successful Broadway musical.

Edison Studios moved to 2826 Decatur Avenue in the Bronx in 1907 and was in operation for eleven years, until Thomas Edison decided to get out of the film business. The Edison Arms is an apartment complex at that address today.

Grand Concourse and 204th Street to reenact a lonely moment Marty has waiting for a bus—there's still a bus stop there today.

Essentially, if you're looking for the vibe of Manhattan's Little Italy in the first half of the twentieth century, you won't actually find it in Little Italy but here in Belmont. In fact, in order to re-create the Little Italy of his childhood, Martin Scorsese ended up shooting much of *Mean Streets* (1973) in Belmont rather than in Little Italy itself.

— Bronx Park Road, The Bronx —

While in the Bronx, Keep an Eye Out for . . .

The Enid A. Haupt Conservatory

at the New York Botanical Garden. It was completed in 1902 but it's featured in Martin Scorsese's *The Age of Innocence* (1993) for a scene set in the 1870s in which Daniel Day-Lewis and Winona Ryder go for a stroll. It also appears in Penny Marshall's *Awakenings* (1990).

QUEENS

Cross over into Queens from the bridges that extend from the Bronx's Throggs Neck peninsula (the neighborhood where the Son of Sam killings took place in 1976–77 and where Spike Lee filmed his movie *Summer of Sam*) and you'll end up in Queens. This borough, the largest by area and the second most populous in New York City, is home today to immigrants from almost every part of the world you can imagine. The United Nations Building may be across the river in Manhattan, but Queens is like a United Nations of its own. Grab a snack of Ecuadorian food in Sunnyside, watch a *futbol* match in a Colombian bar in Jackson Heights, and get a lesson in tai chi at any number of locations in Flushing, the current heart of the Chinese immigrant community in New York, then finish your day with dinner at a Nigerian restaurant in the neighborhood called Jamaica. To get a sense of the diversity you'll find in even just one neighborhood here, watch Frederick Wiseman's documentary *In Jackson Heights*, a three-hour-plus narrator-less cinematic kaleidoscope of the many different immigrant communities that live in the shadow of LaGuardia airport. Wiseman is best known for his "institution documentaries," looking at the operation of one particular business or public service organization, such as *High School*, *Racetrack*, or *Ex Libris*, which puts the spotlight on Manhattan's New York Public Library. *In Jackson Heights* does the same but for an entire neighborhood. It's as important a look at twenty-first-century America as you'll find in any film made in this young millennium.

The City of New York literalized Queens's status as the meeting place of the world with the 1964 World's Fair, featuring pavilions representing eighty nations and forty-five companies and shaping much of Flushing Meadows Corona Park. In *Iron Man 2* (2010), the layout of the World's Fair site represents the chemical composition of a new element billionaire industrialist Howard Stark discovered and that his son, Tony—Robert Downey Jr.'s Iron Man—will finally create as a power source for his super-suit. In the center of the park stands the Unisphere, built for the 1964 fair. On a 20-foot pedestal, it's a 120-foot-tall steel globe representing our planet with its continents

Will Smith and Tommy Lee Jones's extraterrestrial battlers face down hostile aliens at the Queens 1964 World's Fair site in *Men in Black*.

etched into it, and it's where the final battle between Iron Man and the villain played by a scenery-chewing Mickey Rourke takes place. The New York State Pavilion's Observation Towers right nearby look like flying saucers skewered on toothpick-skinny support structures, so in the film *Men in Black* (1997) it was revealed that these circular platforms actually are alien saucers and the entire 1964 World's Fair was staged to provide cover for humanity's first contact with extraterrestrial life. In the film, a rogue alien then steals one of the flying saucers and crashes it into the Unisphere, slicing right through it. Queens is even the place where extraterrestrial life chooses to settle.

FOREST HILLS STADIUM

1 Tennis Place

Right near the Unisphere in Forest Hills you'll find the USTA Billie Jean King National Tennis Center, where the US Open takes place every August and September. This massive facility was built well after the Forest Hills tennis championship depicted in Alfred Hitchcock's *Strangers on a Train*, however. The climactic match that Guy Haines (Farley Granger) plays as quickly as possible so that he can catch the train back to (the fictional) Metcalf, New Jersey, and stop the man who murdered his wife from planting evidence that would incriminate him there, was filmed at the West Side Tennis Club's Forest Hills Stadium. The parallel editing, or crosscutting, between the match and the villain's illicit activities is pure genius. For the long shots of the match, Hitchcock filmed footage of the Davis Cup finals held here in August 1950, then re-created the match for close-ups with Granger in California. The US Open, probably the event Hitchcock is trying to evoke in *Strangers on a Train*, was held here at Forest Hills Stadium annually until 1977. It still stands, and is the site of many concerts each summer.

Tennis plays a huge role in the plot of *Strangers on a Train* because Guy Haines (Farley Granger, pictured here with Ruth Roman) has to play a match at the Forest Hills Stadium while his nemesis, Bruno Antony (Robert Walker), plants evidence incriminating him in the murder of his wife.

Where to Drink:

Neir's Tavern

If you're looking for a place to cool down after taking in a concert at Forest Hills Stadium, head south to the Queens neighborhood of Woodhaven and grab a drink at Neir's Tavern. One of the oldest bars in America, Neir's has been serving drinks to Queens patrons since 1829, with breaks of a few years here and there when it had to close (including during Prohibition). Open for drinks and pub food today, though, Martin Scorsese shot several pivotal scenes in *Goodfellas* (1990) at Neir's. The moment gangster Henry Hill (Ray Liotta) describes the crew Robert De Niro's Jimmy Conway has put together to execute the biggest cash heist in American history takes place at Neir's, as does their celebration when they think they've gotten away with it. But it's during that celebration that Conway realizes he's going to have to "whack" Morrie (Chuck Low), the wig salesman who first gave them the tip to set up the big score. Scorsese shoots this moment with just a slight bit of slow motion to emphasize the wheels that are turning in Conway's brain as he stares at Morrie.

Robert De Niro's Jimmy Conway assembles his crew for the Lufthansa heist at Neir's Tavern in *Goodfellas*—and his paranoia in its aftermath grows here when he sees how casually his crew has been spending the money they stole.

JFK AIRPORT

The criminal caper in question was the Lufthansa heist. Conway and Hill had been shaking down various airline officials at JFK airport's cargo terminals—for "protection fees"—for years. But when Conway got wind of a huge shipment of cash being sent back to America from US servicemen and women stationed in West Germany who were having their dollars converted to Deutschmarks, it seemed like a perfect opportunity to lift some untraceable greenbacks. *Goodfellas* depicts true events, even if the names have been changed (Conway's name in real life was James Burke), as retold in Henry Hill's account to the film's eventual screenwriter Nicholas Pileggi in Pileggi's book *Wiseguy*. The score turned out to be even bigger than they ever dreamed, the largest in American history at that time, with over $5 million in cash and almost a $1 million more in jewelry. It prompted one of the biggest crackdowns on the Mafia by the federal government to that point and it was investigated for decades, with the latest conviction coming in 2014. As Conway becomes ever more obsessed with covering his tracks, he orders the deaths of virtually everyone else involved, a sequence of murders Scorsese sets to the piano-led section of Derek & the Dominos' "Layla."

For less bloody events set at JFK airport, fire up Stuart Rosenberg's delightful 1969 romantic comedy *The April Fools*, starring Jack Lemmon, Catherine Deneuve, and Peter Lawford. Lemmon's Howard races to JFK's TWA Flight Center, the extraordinary modernist terminal designed by legendary architect Eero Saarinen. He's just left his wife (Sally Kellerman) and he knows that Deneuve's Catherine has just left her husband, Lawford's Ted, Howard's old boss. Howard and Catherine shared a deep connection, and he finally realizes it. As he races down the red-carpeted, tubelike hallways in the TWA Flight Center (hallways that are as emblematic of JFK airport as anything on the sprawling site), he encounters Ted, who knows his wife is leaving him but is hell-bent on stopping her leaving with Howard.

It's down that same red-carpeted hallway where the finale of Ang Lee's *The Wedding Banquet* (1993) takes place. Wai-Tung (Winston Chao) is a gay man living in New York with his partner

Simon. He agrees to marry a Chinese woman to help her get a green card to stay in the United States, but when his parents get wind of his impending nuptials they fly all the way to America from Taiwan to throw a massive traditional wedding feast for Wai-Tung. By the end of the movie, the secret is out and Wai-Tung's father (Sihung Lung) realizes his son is gay. How he feels about this, and whether or not he will accept his son, is indicated in these final moments at the TWA Flight Center. Since Trans-World Airlines folded in late 2001, the Flight Center has remained unused and empty, though the big red-letter illuminated TWA sign always remains lit above it. After a years' long refurbishment, the iconic Flight Center reopened as the TWA Hotel in 2019.

ROCK, ROCK, ROCKAWAY BEACH

Another great place to stay if you have an overnight layover at JFK is at a hotel in the peaceful neighborhood of Rockaway Beach, part of the razor-thin Rockaway Peninsula that juts out into the Atlantic just south of the airport. It has the loveliest beach in all of New York City—all the better because the hour-long train ride from Manhattan discourages many city dwellers from planting their beach towels and umbrellas here. On many a day it feels like you have the whole beach to yourself. That feeling in Rockaway Beach of being part of the city but in a world all its own is captured perfectly in *Radio Days*, where Woody Allen's narrator Joe (Seth Green) grows up in the late 1930s and early 1940s.

While in Queens, Keep an Eye Out for . . .

The Museum of the Moving Image

in the neighborhood of Astoria. They have rotating exhibitions featuring props, drawings, and all kinds of behind-the-scenes ephemera from classic movies. The museum itself sits in a building that used to be part of Kaufman Astoria Studios, which is still nestled up against it and remains a working movie studio, with New York City's only backlot. Parts of *Goodfellas* and *Carlito's Way* have been filmed here, as well as the first two Marx Brothers movies: *The Cocoanuts* (1929) and *Animal Crackers* (1930). Travel farther south and west and in the neighborhood of Long Island City and you'll find Silvercup Studios, on the rooftop of which Connor MacLeod (Christopher Lambert) has his final duel with the Kurgan (Clancy Brown) in *Highlander* (1986).

STATEN ISLAND

The Rockaway Peninsula juts out into the Atlantic like an index finger pointing at the least populous of all of New York City's boroughs, Staten Island. Full to this day of working-class New Yorkers, Staten Island features some of the cheapest rents in the city: in part due to how difficult commuting to the island is. The most popular way for people in Staten Island to get to Manhattan is via the Staten Island ferry, memorably included in Mike Nichols's *Working Girl* (1988) as the way Melanie Griffith's Tess would commute to downtown Manhattan for her Wall Street job back and forth each day. Her job may be on Wall Street, but her hair is pure Staten Island. The island's not a place for glamour, a notion Tess reinforces when she celebrates her thirtieth birthday by eating a cupcake on the ferry—a journey which takes about twenty-five minutes each way—during her journey to work. Staten Island has been home to many immigrant strivers first making their home here after arriving in New York.

Charles Boyer's culinary connoisseur Victor Velasco orders a round of ouzo in *Barefoot in the Park*. Mildred Natwick's Ethel finds she can't make a fist after drinking too much ouzo.

A bit of the island's diversity is reflected in *Barefoot in the Park*, when Charles Boyer's gourmand Victor Velasco takes Jane Fonda's, Robert Redford's, and Mildred Natwick's characters to a rough-and-tumble Albanian restaurant there. Redford's buttoned-up Paul isn't sure what to make of the place, and is embarrassed when Fonda's Corie dances with the belly dancer and lustily joins in on the Albanian chant "Shama Shama El Ma Camama."

The Staten Island ferry features in the 1968 romantic comedy *Sweet November*, starring Sandy Dennis, Anthony Newley, and Theodore Bikel.

BROOKLYN

Travel across the Verrazano-Narrows Bridge from Staten Island and you'll wind up in the last and most populous of New York City's boroughs: "Brooklyn, where anything can happen . . . and usually does," according to the scene-setting onscreen text at the beginning of *Arsenic and Old Lace* (1944). Brooklyn was its own city with its own mayor until it consolidated with the other boroughs into New York City in 1898, and, with the obvious exception of Manhattan, it's the one in which the greatest number of films is set.

Brooklyn is first and foremost a place to live, and as Manhattan became more and more overcrowded, and more and more expensive, Brooklyn took in the spillover. One thinks that the family of Cher's Loretta in *Moonstruck*, the Castorinis,

Frank Capra shot *Arsenic and Old Lace* on a soundstage, which makes sense given that this adaptation of a play takes place largely in one room. But there's a matte-painting backdrop of the Brooklyn Bridge. The Gothic arches of the bridge's stone tower nearest to Brooklyn are clearly visible, to give some atmosphere.

might originally have lived on the Lower East Side but moved to their brownstone at 19 Cranberry Street in Brooklyn Heights, a neighborhood close to the Brooklyn Bridge, when they had more money to escape the tenement life. Today Brooklyn Heights is even more expensive than many parts of Manhattan, so the Castorinis would have had the last laugh.

About a fifteen-minute drive northwest from the Castorinis' brownstone in *Moonstruck* you'll find yourself in the neighborhood of Williamsburg, where the Nolans, the Irish American family who are the subjects of *A Tree Grows in Brooklyn* (1945), settled in the early 1900s. They live on Bogart Street, a narrow residential street stretching from Flushing Avenue to 10 Eyck Street. It's easily accessible by subway. The Grand Street L train station is just a short walking distance away. It'll take thirty minutes to walk from Bogart Street to the School Settlement Association, located at 120 Jackson Street. This settlement house, a place where kids can have nurturing out-of-school experiences, is where the original ailanthus, or "Tree of Heaven," grew that inspired author Betty Smith's 1943 novel.

The *New York Times* reported in 2008 that the brownstone at 19 Cranberry Street that served as the home for Cher's Loretta and her parents in *Moonstruck* had sold for $4 million.

Spotlight on Do the Right Thing (1989)

Plenty of streets in New York City have been renamed in honor of
movie stars, jazz legends, or athletes, but *Do the Right Thing* (1989)
was the first film to receive that honor—actually the first work of art
altogether. *Do the Right Thing Way* is just one block in the Bedford-
Stuyvesant neighborhood, on Stuyvesant Avenue between Lexington
Avenue and Quincy Street, and it was where Spike Lee filmed his
color-splashed 1989 magnum opus about racial tensions boiling
over on one extremely sizzling summer day. Lee hosted a block
party here to celebrate the film's twenty-fifth anniversary in 2014.
Do the Right Thing is a quintessential New York movie because it's
about an ever-relevant New York problem: How can you ensure
that people from so many different backgrounds, races, and cultures
who are thrown together in such tight proximity coexist in mutual
respect rather than mutual distrust?

Lee himself played Mookie, a delivery guy who works at Sal's
Pizza Parlor. His boss Sal (Danny Aiello) is kind in many ways
but clueless about his own racist biases. The film shows how
prejudices can spiral out of control.

Gentle giant Radio Raheem (Bill Nunn) is also brash and unapologetic in his wearing of brass knuckles that read "Love" and "Hate" and in blasting his boom box—the unjust violence he faces makes him the film's most tragic character.

So much of *Do the Right Thing* is filmed outside on Stuyvesant Street itself that the Bed-Stuy neighborhood becomes a character in the movie. Characters, like those played by Ossie Davis and Ruby Dee, mingle outside because they don't have AC, or at least their AC doesn't work well, on this hot, hot day.

The Taking of Pelham One Two Three takes place entirely in Manhattan but all the scenes on the underground tracks were actually filmed at the closed Court Street Station in Brooklyn.

OVER AND UNDER

The subway is a way of life if you live in Brooklyn, especially since many of Brooklyn's residents work in Manhattan. It's cut down on the amount of traffic that runs through the city as a whole, but in Brooklyn, with many of its streets wider already than those in Manhattan and having tree-lined, park-like medians, the subway's really helped to give whole neighborhoods a more laid-back, pedestrian-friendly atmosphere. A visit to the New York Transit Museum in Brooklyn Heights, near the brownstone where Cher's family in *Moonstruck*, the Castorinis, live, gives you a sense of how the subway got started. The first underground line opened in 1904. Each year during the holidays, several vintage trains from the earlier history of the subway are taken

The *One Two Three* of the title of *The Taking of Pelham One Two Three* refers to the time that particular subway train in the movie leaves its origin station, at Pelham in the Bronx, 1:23 p.m.

out of mothballs and run from Brooklyn to Manhattan to give you a sense of what riding the subway would have been like way back when. A visit to the New York Transit Museum at 99 Schermerhorn Street, Brooklyn, includes the abandoned Court Street subway station, which is the station and nearby track where Robert Shaw's hijacker stops the subway train he's taken over at gunpoint in *The Taking of Pelham One Two Three* (1974)—though the action onscreen takes place in Manhattan.

The first elevated train was opened in Manhattan in 1868, and the construction of high, overpass-like structures to place rapid-transit lines in the air was initially more feasible than building tunnels underground. One of these elevated lines runs along

Ruthless cop Popeye Doyle (Gene Hackman) commandeers a citizen's car to chase down a criminal riding above him on the subway in *The French Connection*.

much of Eighty-Sixth Street in the Brooklyn neighborhood of Bensonhurst. Underneath this particular elevated track, beginning at the intersection of Eighty-Sixth Street and Stillwell Avenue, Gene Hackman's brutal cop Popeye Doyle drives a 1971 Pontiac LeMans in *The French Connection* to chase down a perp riding the subway. He races through the traffic, endangering countless lives in the process, keeping close on the tail of the subway train he's chasing all the way to Sixty-Second Street and New Utrecht Avenue.

You can reenact Doyle's route yourself to this day, though please drive responsibly. On the route, you can stop off at Eighty-Sixth Street and Bay Twenty-Third Street for a bite at Lenny's Pizza, where John Travolta's Tony Manero orders a couple slices at the outside counter in *Saturday Night Fever* (1977) then struts his stuff down the street eating his lunch while the Bee Gees' "Stayin' Alive" pulses on the soundtrack. Lenny's remains in business, for indoor dining or to order a slice outside like Manero does. Nearby, at 7305 Fifth Avenue, is the paint store where Manero works his dead-end job; it's changed a bit since then

While in Brooklyn, Keep an Eye Out for . . .

The famous street-level view of the Manhattan Bridge that became the poster for Sergio Leone's *Once Upon a Time in America* (1984). You can see it for yourself by looking north on Washington Street, where it intersects Water Street.

Saturday Night Fever was based on a 1976 *New York* magazine article by Nik Cohn called "Tribal Rites of the New Saturday Night." Cohn later admitted his story was heavily fictionalized, though he said he felt his editors should have realized that.

Tony Manero likes to showboat on the dance floor, but he becomes a better person when he learns to dance with a partner (Karen Lynn Gorney), even giving up the trophy he wins in a dance contest to a more-deserving Puerto Rican couple.

but it's still a hardware store, so a good place to pick up some 2 x 4s after you've had double-decker slices.

The most memorable scenes in *Saturday Night Fever* take place on the dance floor, of course. The movie cemented the Bee Gees as superstars. The dynamic dance sequences, shot on the kind of illuminated grid floor so popular in discotheques of the '70s, took place at the 2001 Odyssey nightclub. It was a very real club and stood at 802 Sixty-Fourth Street. But as disco faded in popularity, so did the 2001 Odyssey's fortunes. After being turned into a gay bar for a few years it was demolished, and today an East Asian holistic medicine and allergy clinic exists at the site.

CONEY ISLAND

Coney Island is New York City's playground. Since the 1870s, when the railroad was extended to this peninsula on the southern edge of Brooklyn, New Yorkers have loved journeying to Coney Island because it's convenient enough to the heart of the city but feels far enough removed to be a world unto itself. People come here for the beach and for the many amusement park rides along its boardwalk. The most famous of these is the wooden roller coaster, the Cyclone, which

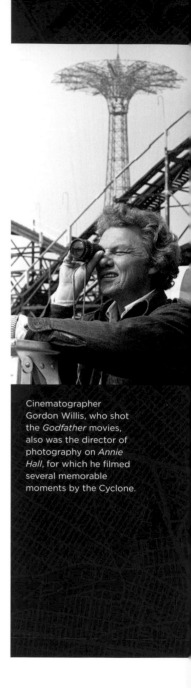

Cinematographer Gordon Willis, who shot the *Godfather* movies, also was the director of photography on *Annie Hall*, for which he filmed several memorable moments by the Cyclone.

Jared Leto's Harry Goldfarb walks the boardwalk on Coney Island in *Requiem for a Dream*.

had a starring role in *Annie Hall*. Young Alvy Singer is shown to have grown up in a house which, oddly enough, stands within the wooden superstructure of the coaster. Perhaps the incessant rattling of the cars and screams of the riders account for Singer's perpetual neuroses even unto adulthood. While they're having a welcome home party there in 1945 for his cousin, the house shakes from the Cyclone.

There's an aura of sadness at Coney Island, though. The kind that often seems to haunt places that are meant to be fun, particularly amusement parks. Those parks at Coney Island have been magnets for a seedy crowd, including drug pushers and gangs, over the decades. In Walter Hill's 1979 cult crime film *The Warriors*, a gang with that name make their home on Coney Island—the entire plot of the movie is about them fighting their way from the farthest northern part of the Bronx all the way back to Coney Island following a gang meet-up gone wrong. The resolution of the movie takes place on Coney Island's boardwalk. Likewise, the boardwalk features in Darren Aronofsky's *Requiem for a Dream* (2000). Most of that film takes place in the eastern part of Coney Island, called Brighton Beach after a resort that was opened here in the 1870s that tried to replicate the seaside charm of the resort town of Brighton in England. Brighton Beach is home to a large population of Russian emigrés in New York City. It's in this neighborhood where lovelorn softie Leonard (Joaquin Phoenix) lives with his Russian-Jewish family in *Two Lovers* (2009), as a man infatuated with one woman (Gwyneth Paltrow) and fails to appreciate the love of another (Vinessa Shaw) who ultimately cares for him even that much more. In the final scene, Leonard goes at night to the water's edge on Coney Island, having just had his heart broken once and for all. He stares out at the sea, the shining lights of the boardwalk and its many amusements behind him, an ironic contrast of mirth and joy to his deep sorrow.

That palpable sadness you feel at Coney Island is also powerfully evoked by Steven Spielberg near the end of *A.I.: Artificial Intelligence*, the sci-fi retelling of Pinocchio he worked on with Stanley Kubrick before the latter filmmaker's death in 1999. The robot David (Haley Joel Osment), who's been fashioned to look like a young boy, yearns, in fact, to be a real boy. With his talking teddy bear robot companion Teddy, they take a submarine to visit the Blue Fairy at the underwater site of what was once Coney Island—the arctic ice caps having completely melted, the ocean has covered the Statue of Liberty and much of New York City, including the former amusement park at Coney Island. It turns out, the Blue Fairy is just a statue that happens to be located in the wreckage of the old rides that stood on the site. But, statue or not, it's here where David can finally ask the Blue Fairy to turn him into a real boy.

Some of Coney Island's best depictions are in the silent era. Perhaps because it's such a raucous place, it comes across better when you can just see it and not hear it. And it was not long after the introduction of sound in movies of the late 1920s that the amusements here began their long decay. At its zenith, though, you can see

Fatty Arbuckle goes on a ride at Luna Park in the comic short subject *Coney Island* from 1917.

Coney Island in King Vidor's *The Crowd* (1928). On the boardwalk, John (James Murray) and Mary (Eleanor Boardman) first spend time together and begin to fall in love. John's father always told him he would be something special—but as others had noted, it would take a lot in life to stand out from the crowd. And John, when he meets Mary, is only working as an office schlub in one of an endless matrix of desks at Manhattan's Atlas Insurance Company. That's hardly standing out from the crowd. Nor is enjoying their recreation at Coney Island alongside thousands of others doing the same. But despite their fun lacking distinction, they still connect, even in the midst of the throngs—maybe it's something like what Jordan Baker says in *The Great Gatsby*: "I love big parties, they're so intimate. At small parties there isn't any privacy." Maybe getting lost in the crowd isn't such a bad thing after all.

More than a decade earlier, in 1917's twenty-five-minute short subject *Coney Island*, Buster Keaton and Fatty Arbuckle go for a day of mirth at Luna Park—the main amusement park at Coney Island from 1903 to 1944. (A Luna Park reopened at Coney Island in 2010, after a previous version had folded.) They go beachcombing, watch a parade, perform feats of strength, get overly competitive on the famed "witching waves" ride, eat ice cream, get into a fight, and end up soaked from the "old mill"—a mishap that results in them donning women's clothing. Harold Lloyd has a similar disaster in *Speedy* (1928), when he ruins his suit at Coney Island by leaning against wet paint.

By the time Arbuckle and Keaton made their film, Coney Island had already gone through several heydays and periods of reinvention. One structure that went on to have a huge cinematic legacy was the Elephantine Colossus that used to stand on Coney Island. With thirty-one rooms and serving as a hotel and concert hall, it was a seven-story building in the shape of a giant elephant—trunk, tusks, and all. It was the inspiration for the giant elephant in which Nicole Kidman's courtesan Satine lives in *Moulin Rouge!* (2001) and, just like that architectural pachyderm located at the iconic dancehall in Paris, the Elephantine Colossus of Coney Island was also used as a brothel. It stood here from 1885 to 1896, when it burned down in a fire. It was such a landmark that there was real sadness when it went up in flames, even making the cover of the October 1896 issue of *The Illustrated American* with the headline "A Coney Island Tragedy: Burning of The Historic Elephant." But if you want to see a surviving example of the Elephantine Colossus, you're in luck: its designer, the architect James V. Lafferty, built another one that survives. It's called Lucy the Elephant and it stands in Margate City, New Jersey, where it has been since it was built in 1881, though it's about half the size of the one that stood at Coney Island. When you visit you can live out your *Moulin Rouge!* fantasies.

Coney Island is the ideal spot to end our cinematic tour of New York because it makes literal something that's true all across the Big Apple: this city is *fun*. You feel an energy when you're in New York City—as if you can do anything, be anybody, and achieve whatever

Buster Keaton demonstrates his muscle power in a feat of strength in *Coney Island*—unfortunately, his comedy partner Fatty Arbuckle gets caught up in the strong man act.

dreams you desire and have fun doing it. It's similar to the feeling we sometimes get when we're thrilled and inspired by a great movie. Visiting New York feels like you've stepped through the movie screen and into a heightened world where anything is possible. The only question is: What will you do first?

INDEX

ACKNOWLEDGMENTS

This book wasn't just a labor of love, it actually caused me to fall in love that much more deeply with New York City. I've never been more enamored with this extraordinary city that I've called home for the past eleven years than I've been while writing this book—so, first and foremost, thanks must be paid to the more than eight million people who give this city its heartbeat.

I'm so grateful to Cindy De La Hoz at Running Press for believing in me during all stages of the creation of this book and offering invaluable advice to make it sharper and smarter. Also at Running Press I wish to thank publisher Kristin Kiser, publicist Seta Zink, and designer Melissa Gerber. Thanks to Aaron Spiegeland at Parham Santana and John Malahy at Turner Classic Movies for their incisive edits and suggestions. And much appreciation also goes to their TCM colleagues Jennifer Dorian, Heather Margolis, Genevieve Tobin, Kendel White, Sean Cameron, and Susana Zepeda Cagan.

What an honor to have this book exist in partnership with TCM, a channel I have on my TV virtually all the time and has been such an inextricable part of my life and daily routine for years. Appearing on TCM for the first time in 2017 to cohost a night of programming with Ben Mankiewicz was one of the great joys of my career to date. Ben is the real deal: someone deeply knowledgeable enough to edit his scripts in real-time before the cameras roll, and a kind, funny, and encouraging friend.

A massive thank you must be paid to the many friends who encouraged me throughout the writing of this book and added their own suggestions for films and locations to be featured within: Tom Brook and his extraordinary crew for the BBC World News show *Talking Movies* deserve special thanks—especially Anthony Svatek, Tristan Daley, Andrew Blum, Emma De'Ath, and Emma Jones—for turning part of what was meant to be a celebratory dinner for that show's twentieth anniversary into a brainstorming session for this book; my best friend Jeremy Berman, the single most knowledgeable cinephile I've ever known, for his sage counsel throughout; Ed Casey, who put me in touch with Running Press in the first place and without whom I would not have written this book at all; and my charming, supportive, super hard-working colleagues at IndieWire, where I'm lucky enough to call myself managing editor.

But most of all, I must give my most profound thanks to my mom, Dianne, an accomplished writer herself who has literally given me everything. It's because of her that I fell in love with the movies, with New York City, and with the art of writing, in the first place. I owe her my worldview, my inventory of interests, my enthusiasm for the very things I love so much—oh, and that little matter of my life as well. This is my seventh book, but I can say definitively that, for my mom and me, it is one of the most meaningful. So much so, that I can only sum up the wonderful experience of publishing it with this: "Made it, Ma! Top of the world!"

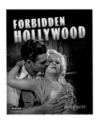

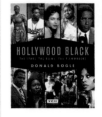

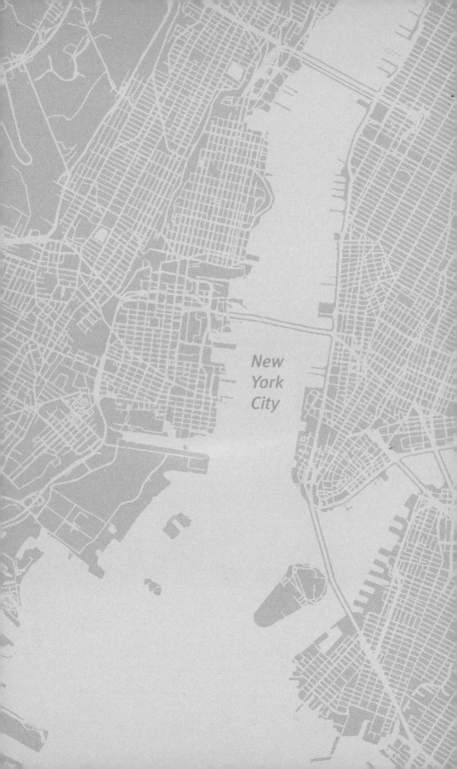
New York
City